Readings in Literature for Upper Grades

PR

READINGS IN LITERATURE

FOR UPPER GRADES

SELECTED AND EDITED. BY

T. ADRIAN ÇURTIS

PRINCIPAL IN THE PUBLIC SCHOOLS, NEW YORK CITY

NEW YORK

CHARLES E. MERRILL COMPANY

1915

PREFACE

BECAUSE of the importance of the subject of Reading in Elementary School curricula, much thought and attention have been given by prominent educators to devising methods whereby the beginner may be taught to master the printed page. The various methods invented and put into operation have resulted in rapid progress in the scientific manner of presenting and developing the beginnings of this art. In the lower grades, the advance that has been made in the teaching of reading is satisfactory from every standpoint. While the mechanical side of the art has been provided for, the content side has not been neglected.

Unfortunately we cannot view with the same complacence the conditions that exist in connection with reading in the upper grades. There we are confronted with the two-fold problem, first, of continuing the process of aiding the pupils in the matter of oral expression, and second, of leading them to a real appreciation of the masterpieces of literature. No matter how excellent may be the results obtained in the mechanics of reading, unless the pupils are inspired with a love for good books, we have failed to accomplish the most important aim of the course. This double problem makes it necessary to select the reading matter for the upper grades with the greatest care. If one or two long selections are studied intensively during a term, the pupils are not brought in touch with the variety of topics and styles that is essential to the awakening of a broad, lively, permanent interest in books. On the other hand, if the ordinary class reader with a great number of short selections is used, the results are not satisfactory because the incomplete selections do not make the required appeal to pupils, nor do they, as a rule, lend themselves to the analytical study that is necessary to an intelligent appreciation of the classics.

This book has been planned to act as a kind of connecting link between the class reader and the long masterpiece. In choosing the material for it, the following things have been kept in mind: first, that a variety of topics must be presented; second, that the material must be interesting in itself; third, that the material must present no abnormal difficulty in the correct oral rendering of it; fourth, that the selections must be such that the teacher will find it profitable to let the pupils see something of the workmanship required in producing a masterpiece of literature. Seven of the prose selections are given in their entirety; two are extracts from longer stories. The complete pieces lend themselves to an analytical study that should be beneficial to the pupils in their composition work. The treatment outlined under the "Notes and Suggestions" at the end of each selection has been worked out with the double purpose in view, first, of training the pupils in placing an intelligent valuation on the work of the masters, and second, of showing them the importance of the mechanical side of the art of expression. Not all of the allusions have been explained in the notes. Where a knowledge of the meaning of the allusion is essential to an understanding of the passage, an explanatory note is given at the end. In regard to all other allusions, historical references and the like, it is

advisable to have the pupils feel the necessity for looking
them up in appropriate books of reference. Training in the
use of reference books is a valuable asset for the pupils.

The selections in this book may well be made the basis
for further work with library books. The more closely the
reading of library books is supervised by the teacher, the
better are the results obtained from such reading. If the
pupils have read in class the extract from Owen Johnson's
school story, then suggest the reading at home of such books
as "Stalky and Co." or "Tom Brown"; and require a report
on their home reading. Let them know what to look for and
that you expect a definite response from them and you will
increase wonderfully the interest in this important part of
the work. Suggestions as to supplementary home reading
will also be found at the end of each selection. They are
suggestions only. The enthusiastic teacher will change and
add to this list according to his or her taste in reading and
will thus give to the work the individualism which is so necessary to its success.

In attempting to create a taste for literature, the engender-
ing and nurturing of a love for poetry is an essential part of
the work. To be successful in this regard, considerable skill
and enthusiasm are required on the part of the teacher. We
cannot expect children of elementary school age to be able,
unaided, to appreciate the beauties of lyric poetry. If, however, they are placed in the correct emotional attitude by the
methods employed, it is possible to inspire them with a lasting
love for poetry. Where the lyrics are narrative in form, the
problem of arousing interest is not so difficult, for the story
told makes the selection easier for them to understand.

Where the poem is purely lyrical, the teacher must be sure that the children see and understand the implied meanings as well as those expressed. It is important for the teacher to bring to the attention of the pupils, those facts in the life of the poet that may aid them in their interpretation of the poem. It is advisable to have at least a part of the memory work for the grade taken from the poems given here. Of course, the process of memorizing must not begin until the poem has been studied, understood and appreciated.

Grateful acknowledgement for permission to use copyrighted material is hereby made to the following publishers: Charles Scribner's Sons for "San Francisco,—A Modern Cosmopolis" by Robert Louis Stevenson; Doubleday, Page and Co. for "Art and the Bronco" by O. Henry and for the selection from "The Varmint" by Owen Johnson.

T. A. C.

TABLE OF CONTENTS

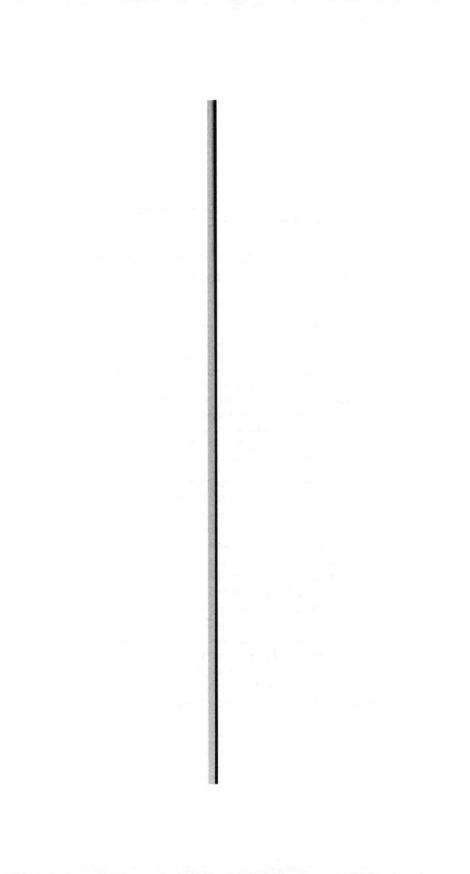

READINGS IN LITERATURE

THE LEGEND OF SLEEPY HOLLOW

(Found among the papers of the late Diedrich Knickerbocker)

BY WASHINGTON IRVING

WASHINGTON IRVING was born in New York in 1783 and died in Tarrytown in 1859. He was one of the earliest of our American writers. His fame is based on his historical works and his short sketches. A great many years of his life were spent abroad in travel and in the diplomatic service of the United States. His writings are characterized by a graceful, engaging style and a genial, kindly humor. Irving was the first of our writers to use the short story as a distinct literary form.

The Legend of Sleepy Hollow is one of the stories in " The Sketch Book," which was published in 1818.

IN the bosom of one of those spacious coves which indent the eastern shore of the Hudson, at that broad expansion of the river denominated by the ancient Dutch navigators the Tappan Zee, and where they always pru-
5 dently shortened sail, and implored the protection of St. Nicholas when they crossed, there lies a small market town or rural port, which by some is called Greensburgh, but which is more generally and properly known by the name of Tarry Town. This name was given it, we are
10 told, in former days, by the good housewives of the adjacent country, from the inveterate propensity of their husbands to linger about the village tavern on market days. Be that as it may, I do not vouch for the fact, but merely advert to it, for the sake of being precise and
15 authentic. Not far from this village, perhaps about

two miles, there is a little valley, or rather lap of land among high hills, which is one of the quietest places in the whole world. A small brook glides through it, with just murmur enough to lull one to repose; and the occa-
5 sional whistle of a quail, or tapping of a woodpecker, is almost the only sound that ever breaks in upon the uniform tranquility.

I recollect that, when a stripling, my first exploit in squirrel-shooting was in a grove of tall walnut-trees that
10 shades one side of the valley. I had wandered into it at noon time when all nature is peculiarly quiet, and was startled by the roar of my own gun, as it broke the Sabbath stillness around, and was prolonged and reverberated by the angry echoes. If ever I should wish for a
15 retreat whither I might steal from the world and its distractions, and dream quietly away the remnant of a troubled life, I know of none more promising than this little valley.

From the listless repose of the place, and the peculiar
20 character of its inhabitants, who are descendants from the original Dutch settlers, this sequestered glen has long been known by the name of Sleepy Hollow, and its rustic lads are called the Sleepy Hollow boys throughout all the neighboring country. A drowsy, dreamy influence seems
25 to hang over the land, and to pervade the very atmosphere. Some say that the place was bewitched by a high German doctor, during the early days of the settlement; others, that an old Indian chief, the prophet or wizard of his tribe, held his powwows there before the
30 country was discovered by Master Hendrick Hudson. Certain it is, the place still continues under the sway of some witching power, that holds a spell over the minds of the good people, causing them to walk in a continual reverie. They are given to all kinds of marvelous beliefs;
35 are subject to trances and visions; and frequently see

strange sights, and hear music and voices in the air.
The whole neighborhood abounds with local tales,
haunted spots, and twilight superstitions; stars shoot
and meteors glare oftener across the valley than in any
5 other part of the country, and the nightmare, with her
whole ninefold, seems to make it the favorite scene of her
gambols.

The dominant spirit, however, that haunts this en-
chanted region, and seems to be commander-in-chief of
10 all the powers of the air, is the apparition of a figure on
. horseback without a head. It is said by some to be the
ghost of a Hessian trooper, whose head had been carried
away by a cannon ball, in some nameless battle during
the Revolutionary War; and who is ever and anon seen
15 by the country folk, hurrying along in the gloom of
night, as if on the wings of the wind. His haunts are not
confined to the valley, but extend at times to the adjacent
roads, and especially to the vicinity of a church at no
great distance. Indeed, certain of the most authen-
20 tic historians of those parts, who have been careful in
collecting and collating the floating facts concerning this
specter, allege that the body of the trooper having been
buried in the churchyard, the ghost rides forth to the
scene of battle in nightly quest of his head; and that the
25 rushing speed with which he sometimes passes along the
Hollow, like a midnight blast, is owing to his being be-
lated, and in a hurry to get back to the churchyard before
daybreak.

Such is the general purport of this legendary super-
30 stition, which has furnished materials for many a wild
story in that region of shadows; and the specter is known
at all the country firesides, by the name of The Headless
Horseman of Sleepy Hollow.

It is remarkable, that the visionary propensity I have
35 mentioned is not confined to the native inhabitants of

the valley, but it is unconsciously imbibed by everyone
who resides there for a time. However wide awake they
may have been before they entered that sleepy region,
they are sure, in a little time, to inhale the witching
5 influence of the air, and begin to grow imaginative—to
dream dreams and see apparitions.

I mention this peaceful spot with all possible laud,
for it is in such little retired Dutch valleys, found here
and there enbosomed in the great state of New York,
10 that population, manners, and customs, remain fixed;
while the great torrent of migration and improvement,
which is making such incessant changes in other parts of
this restless country, sweeps by them unobserved. They
are like those little nooks of still water, which border a
15 rapid stream; where we may see the straw and bubble
riding quietly at anchor, or slowly revolving in their
mimic harbor, undisturbed by the rush of the passing
current. Though many years have elapsed since I trod
the drowsy shades of Sleepy Hollow, yet I question
20 whether I should not still find the same trees and the
same families vegetating in its sheltered bosom.

In this byplace of nature, there abode, in a remote
period of American history, that is to say, some thirty
years since, a worthy wight of the name of Ichabod
25 Crane, who sojourned, or, as he expressed it, "tarried," in
Sleepy Hollow, for the purpose of instructing the children
of the vicinity. He was a native of Connecticut; a state
which supplies the Union with pioneers for the mind as
well as for the forest, and sends forth yearly its legions
30 of frontier woodsmen and country schoolmasters. The
cognomen of Crane was not inapplicable to his person.
He was tall but exceedingly lank, with narrow shoulders,
long arms and legs, hands that dangled a mile out of his
sleeves, feet that might have served for shovels and his
35 whole frame most loosely hung together. His head was

small, and flat at top, with huge ears, large green glassy
eyes, and a long snipe nose, so that it looked like a weather-
cock, perched upon a spindle neck, to tell which way the
wind blew.   To see him striding along the profile of a
5 hill on a windy day, with his clothes bagging and fluttering about him, one might have mistaken him for the
genius of famine descending upon the earth, or some
scarecrow eloped from a cornfield.

His schoolhouse was a low building of one large room,
10 rudely constructed of logs; the windows partly glazed,
and partly patched with leaves of old copybooks.   It was
most ingeniously secured at vacant hours by a withe
twisted in the handle of the door, and stakes set against
the window shutters; so that though a thief might get in
15 with perfect ease, he would find some embarrassment in
getting out; an idea most probably borrowed by the
architect, Yost Van Houten, from the mystery of an eel-
pot.   The schoolhouse stood in a rather lonely but pleasant situation, just at the foot of a woody hill, with a brook
20 running close by, and a formidable birch tree growing at
one end of it.   From hence the low murmur of his pupils'
voices, conning over their lessons, might be heard in a
drowsy summer's day, like the hum of a beehive; interrupted now and then by the authoritative voice of the
25 master, in the tone of menace or command; or, peradventure, by the appalling sound of the birch, as he urged
some tardy loiterer along the flowery path of knowledge.
Truth to say, he was a conscientious man, and ever bore
in mind the golden maxim, "spare the rod and spoil the
30 child."—Ichabod Crane's scholars certainly were not
spoiled.

I would not have it imagined, however, that he was
one of those cruel potentates of the school, who joy in the
smart of their subjects; on the contrary, he administered
35 justice with discrimination rather than severity; taking

the burthen off the backs of the weak and laying it on
those of the strong. Your mere puny stripling that
winced at the least flourish of the rod, was passed by
with indulgence; but the claims of justice were satisfied
5 by inflicting a double portion on some little, tough, wrong-
headed, broad-skirted Dutch urchin, who sulked and
swelled and grew dogged and sullen beneath the birch.
All this he called "doing his duty by their parents," and
he never inflicted a chastisement without following it by
10 the assurance, so consolatory to the smarting urchin, that
"he would remember it and thank him for it the longest
day he had to live."

When school hours were over, he was even the companion and playmate of the larger boys; and on holiday
15 afternoons would convoy some of the smaller ones home,
who happened to have pretty sisters, or good housewives
for mothers, noted for the comforts of the cupboard.
Indeed, it behooved him to keep on good terms with his
pupils. The revenue arising from his school was small,
20 and would have been scarcely sufficient to furnish him
with daily bread, for he was a huge feeder, and though
lank, had the dilating powers of an anaconda; but to help
out his maintenance, he was, according to country custom
in those parts, boarded and lodged at the houses of the
25 farmers, whose children he instructed. With these he
lived successively. a week at a time; thus going the rounds
of the neighborhood with all his worldly effects tied up
in a cotton handkerchief.

That all this might not be too onerous on the purses
30 of his rustic patrons, who are apt to consider the costs of
schooling a grievous burthen, and schoolmasters as
mere drones, he had various ways of rendering himself
both useful and agreeable. He assisted the farmers occasionally in the lighter labors of their farms; helped to
35 make hay; mended the fences; took the horses to water;

drove the cows from the pasture; and cut wood for the
winter fire. He laid aside, too, all the dominant dignity
and absolute sway with which he lorded it in his little
empire, the school, and became wonderfully gentle and
5 ingratiating. He found favor in the eyes of the mothers
by petting the children, particularly the youngest; and
like the lion bold, which whilome so magnanimously the
lamb did hold, he would sit with a child on one knee, and
rock a cradle with his foot for whole hours together.
10   In addition to his other vocations, he was the singing
master of the neighborhood, and picked up many bright
shillings by instructing the young folks in psalmody. It
was a matter of no little vanity to him on Sundays, to
take his station in front of the church gallery, with a band
15 of chosen singers; where, in his own mind, he completely
carried away the palm from the parson. Certain it is,
his voice resounded far above all the rest of the congregation; and there are peculiar quavers still to be heard in
that church, and which may even be heard half a mile off,
20 quite to the opposite side of the mill pond, on a still
Sunday morning, which are said to be legitimately de-
scended from the nose of Ichabod Crane. Thus, by
divers little makeshifts in that ingenious way which is
commonly denominated "by hook and by crook," the
25 worthy pedagogue got on tolerably enough, and was
thought by all who understood nothing of the labor of
head work, to have a wonderfully easy life of it.
    The schoolmaster is generally a man of some impor-
tance in the female circle of a rural neighborhood; being
30 considered a kind of idle gentleman-like personage, of
vastly superior taste and accomplishments to the rough
country swains, and, indeed, inferior in learning only to
the parson. His appearance, therefore, is apt to occasion some little stir at the tea table of a farmhouse, and
35 the addition of a supernumerary dish of cakes or sweet-

meats, or, peradventure, the parade of a silver teapot.
Our man of letters, therefore, was peculiarly happy in
the smiles of all the country damsels. How he would
figure among them in the churchyard, between services
5 on Sundays! gathering grapes for them from the wild
vines that overrun the surrounding trees; reciting for
their amusement all the epitaphs on the tombstones; or
sauntering, with a whole bevy of them, along the banks
of the adjacent mill pond; while the more bashful country
10 bumpkins hung sheepishly back, envying his superior
elegance and address.

From his half itinerant life, also, he was a kind of
traveling gazette, carrying the whole budget of local
gossip from house to house; so that his appearance was
15 always greeted with satisfaction. He was, moreover,
esteemed by the women as a man of great erudition, for
he had read several books quite through, and was a perfect master of Cotton Mather's "History of New England Witchcraft," in which, by the way, he most firmly
20 and potently believed.

He was, in fact, an odd mixture of small shrewdness
and simple credulity. His appetite for the marvelous,
and his powers of digesting it, were equally extraordinary;
and both had been increased by his residence in this spell-
25 bound region. No tale was too gross or monstrous for
his capacious swallow. It was often his delight, after his
school was dismissed in the afternoon, to stretch himself
on the rich bed of clover, bordering the little brook that
whimpered by his schoolhouse, and there con over old
30 Mather's direful tales, until the gathering dusk of evening made the printed page a mere mist before his eyes.
Then, as he wended his way by swamp and stream and
awful woodland, to the farmhouse where he happened to
be quartered, every sound of nature, at that witching hour,
35 fluttered his excited imagination: the moan of the whip-

poor-will from the hillside; the boding cry of the tree
toad, that harbinger of storm; the dreary hooting of the
screech-owl, or the sudden rustling in the thicket, of birds
frightened from their roost. The fireflies, too, which
5 sparkled most vividly in the darkest places, now and then
startled him, as one of uncommon brightness would stream
across his path; and if, by chance, a huge blockhead of a
beetle came winging his blundering flight against him,
the poor varlet was ready to give up the ghost, with the
10 idea that he was struck with a witch's token. His only
resource on such occasions, either to drown thought, or
drive away evil spirits, was to sing psalm tunes;—and the
good people of Sleepy Hollow, as they sat by their doors
of an evening, were often filled with awe, at hearing his
15 nasal melody, "in linked sweetness long drawn out,"
floating from the distant hill, or along the dusky road.

Another of his sources of fearful pleasure was, to pass
long winter evenings with the old Dutch wives, as they
sat spinning by the fire, with a row of apples roasting
20 and sputtering along the hearth, and listen to their
marvelous tales of ghosts and goblins, and haunted fields
and haunted brooks, and haunted bridges and haunted
houses, and particularly of The Headless Horseman, or
Galloping Hessian of the Hollow, as they sometimes
25 called him. He would delight them equally by his anec-
dotes of witchcraft, and of the direful omens and porten-
tous sights and sounds in the air, which prevailed in the
earlier times of Connecticut; and would frighten them
woefully with speculations upon comets and shooting
30 stars; and with the alarming fact that the world did
absolutely turn round, and that they were half the time
topsy-turvy!

But if there was a pleasure in all this, while snugly
cuddling in the chimney corner of a chamber that was all
35 of a ruddy glow from the crackling wood fire, and where,

of course, no specter dared to show his face, it was dearly
purchased by the terrors of his subsequent walk homeward. What fearful shapes and shadows beset his path
amidst the dim and ghastly glare of a snowy night!—With
5 what wistful look did he eye every trembling ray of light
streaming across the waste fields from some distant window! How often was he appalled by some shrub covered with snow, which, like a sheeted specter, beset his
very path! How often did he shrink with curdling awe
10 at the sound of his own steps on the frosty crust beneath
his feet; and dread to look over his shoulder, lest he should
behold some uncouth being tramping close behind him!—
and how often was he thrown into complete dismay by
some rushing blast, howling among the trees, in the idea
15 that it was the Galloping Hessian on one of his nightly
scourings!

All these, however, were mere terrors of the night,
phantoms of the mind that walk in darkness; and though
he had seen many specters in his time, and had been more
20 than once beset by Satan in divers shapes, in his lonely
perambulations, yet daylight put an end to all these evils;
and he would have passed a pleasant life of it, in despite
of the devil and all his works, if his path had not been
crossed by a being that causes more perplexity to mortal
25 man than ghosts, goblins, and the whole race of witches
put together, and that was—a woman.

Among the musical disciples who assembled, one
evening in each week, to receive his instructions in psalmody, was Katrina Van Tassel, the daughter and only
30 child of a substantial Dutch farmer. She was a blooming lass of fresh eighteen; plump as a partridge; ripe and
melting and rosy-cheeked as one of her father's peaches,
and universally famed, not merely for her beauty, but
her vast expectations. She was withal a little of a co-
35 quette, as might be perceived even in her dress, which

was a mixture of ancient and modern fashions, as most
suited to set off her charms. She wore the ornaments of
pure yellow gold, which her great-great-grandmother had
brought over from Saardam; the tempting stomacher of
5 the olden time; and withal a provokingly short petticoat,
to display the prettiest foot and ankle in the country
round.

Ichabod Crane had a soft and foolish heart toward
the sex; and it is not to be wondered at, that so tempting
10 a morsel soon found favor in his eyes, more especially
after he had visited her in her paternal mansion. Old
Baltus Van Tassel was a perfect picture of a thriving,
contented, liberal-hearted farmer. He seldom, it is true,
sent either his eyes or his thoughts beyond the boundaries
15 of his own farm; but within those, everything was snug,
happy and well conditioned. He was satisfied with his
wealth, but not proud of it; and piqued himself upon the
hearty abundance, rather than the style in which he lived.
His stronghold was situated on the banks of the Hudson,
20 in one of those green, sheltered, fertile nooks in which
the Dutch farmers are so fond of nestling. A great elm
tree spread its broad branches over it; at the foot of
which bubbled up a spring of the softest and sweetest
water, in a little well, formed of a barrel; and then stole
25 sparkling away through the grass, to a neighboring brook,
that bubbled along among alders and dwarf willows.
Hard by the farmhouse was a vast barn, that might have
served for a church; every window and crevice of which
seemed bursting forth with the treasures of the farm;
30 the flail was busily resounding within it from morning to
night; swallows and martins skimmed twittering about
the eaves, and rows of pigeons, some with one eye turned
up, as if watching the weather, some with their heads
under their wings or buried in their bosoms, and others
35 swelling and cooing, and bowing about their dames,

were enjoying the sunshine on the roof. Sleek unwieldy
porkers were grunting in the repose and abundance of
their pens; whence sallied forth, now and then, troops
of suckling pigs as if to snuff the air. A stately
5 squadron of snowy geese were riding in an adjoining
pond, convoying whole fleets of ducks; regiments of tur-
keys were gobbling through the farmyard, and guinea
fowls fretting about it, like ill-tempered housewives, with
their peevish discontented cry. Before the barn door
10 strutted the gallant cock, that pattern of a husband, a
warrior, and a fine gentleman, clapping his burnished
wings, and crowing in the pride and gladness of his heart
—sometimes tearing up the earth with his feet; and then
generously calling his ever-hungry family of wives and
15 children to enjoy the rich morsel which he had discovered.

The pedagogue's mouth watered, as he looked upon
this sumptuous promise of luxurious winter fare. In his
devouring mind's eye, he pictured to himself every roast-
ing-pig running about with a pudding in its belly, and
20 an apple in its mouth; the pigeons were snugly put to
bed in a comfortable pie, and tucked in with a coverlet of
crust; the geese were swimming in their own gravy; and
the ducks pairing cosily in dishes, like snug married
couples, with a decent competency of onion sauce. In
25 the porkers he saw carved out the future sleek side of
bacon, and juicy relishing ham; not a turkey but he beheld daintily trussed up, with its gizzard under its wing,
and, peradventure, a necklace of savory sausages; and even
bright chanticleer himself lay sprawling on his back, in a
30 side dish, with uplifted claws, as if craving that quarter
which his chivalrous spirit disdained to ask while living.

As the enraptured Ichabod fancied all this, and as he
rolled his great green eyes over the fat meadow-lands,
the rich fields of wheat, of rye, of buckwheat, and Indian
35 corn, and the orchards burthened with ruddy fruit,

which surrounded the warm tenement of Van Tassel, his heart yearned after the damsel who was to inherit these domains, and his imagination expanded with the idea, how they might be readily turned into cash, and the
5 money invested in immense tracts of wild land, and shingle palaces in the wilderness. Nay, his busy fancy already realized his hopes, and presented to him the blooming Katrina, with a whole family of children, mounted on the top of a wagon loaded with household trumpery, with
10 pots and kettles dangling beneath; and he beheld himself bestriding a pacing mare, with a colt at her heels, setting out for Kentucky, Tennessee, or the Lord knows where.

When he entered the house the conquest of his heart
15 was complete. It was one of those spacious farmhouses, with high-ridged, but lowly sloping roofs, built in the style handed down from the first Dutch settlers; the low projecting eaves forming a piazza along the front, capable of being closed up in bad weather. Under this were hung
20 flails, harness, various utensils of husbandry, and nets for fishing in the neighboring river. Benches were built along the sides for summer use; and a great spinning-wheel at one end, and a churn at the other, showed the various uses to which this important porch might be
25 devoted. From this piazza the wondering Ichabod entered the hall, which formed the center of the mansion, and the place of usual residence. Here rows of resplendent pewter, ranged on a long dresser, dazzled his eyes. In one corner stood a huge bag of wool ready to be spun;
30 in another a quantity of linsey-woolsey just from the loom; ears of Indian corn, and strings of dried apples and peaches, hung in gay festoons along the walls, mingled with the gaud of red peppers; and a door left ajar gave him a peep into the best parlor, where the claw-footed
35 chairs, and dark mahogany tables, shone like mirrors; and-

irons, with their accompanying shovel and tongs, glis-
tened from their covert of asparagus tops; mock-oranges
and conch-shells decorated the mantelpiece; strings of
various colored birds' eggs were suspended above it: a
5 great ostrich egg was hung from the center of the room,
and a corner cupboard, knowingly left open, displayed
immense treasures of old silver and well-mended china.

From the moment Ichabod laid his eyes upon these
regions of delight the peace of his mind was at an end,
10 and his only study was how to gain the affections of the
peerless daughter of Van Tassel. In this enterprise, however, he had more real difficulties than generally fell to
the lot of a knight-errant of yore, who seldom had anything but giants, enchanters, fiery dragons, and such like
15 easily conquered adversaries, to contend with; and had
to make his way merely through gates of iron and brass,
and walls of adamant, to the castle-keep, where the lady
of his heart was confined; all which he achieved as
easily as a man would carve his way to the center of a
20 Christmas pie, and then the lady gave him her hand as
a matter of course. Ichabod, on the contrary, had to
win his way to the heart of a country coquette beset with
a labyrinth of whims and caprices, which were forever
presenting new difficulties and impediments; and he had
25 to encounter a host of fearful adversaries of real flesh and
blood, the numerous rustic admirers, who beset every
portal to her heart; keeping a watchful and angry eye
upon each other, but ready to fly out in the common cause
against any new competitor.

30   Among these the most formidable was a burly, roaring, roistering blade, of the name of Abraham, or, according to the Dutch abbreviation, Brom Van Brunt, the
hero of the country round, which rang with his feats of
strength and hardihood. He was broad-shouldered and
35 double-jointed, with short curly black hair, and a bluff,

but not unpleasant countenance, having a mingled
air of fun and arrogance. From his herculean frame
and great powers of limb, he had received the nickname
of Brom Bones, by which he was universally known. He
5 was famed for great knowledge and skill in horsemanship,
being as dexterous on horseback as a Tartar. He
was foremost at all races and cock-fights; and with the
ascendancy which bodily strength acquires in rustic
life, was the umpire in all disputes, setting his hat on
10 one side, and giving his decision with an air and tone admitting of no gainsay or appeal. He was always ready
for either a fight or a frolic; but had more mischief
than ill-will in his composition; and, with all his over-
bearing roughness there was a strong dash of waggish
15 good humor at bottom. He had three or four boon companions, who regarded him as their model, and at the
head of whom he scoured the country, attending every
scene of feud or merriment for miles round. In cold
weather he was distinguished by a fur cap, surmounted
20 with a flaunting fox's tail; and when the folks at a
country gathering descried this well-known crest at a
distance, whisking about among a squad of hard riders,
they always stood by for a squall. Sometimes his crew
would be heard dashing along past the farmhouses at
25 midnight, with whoop and halloo, like a troop of Don
Cossacks; and the old dames, startled out of their sleep,
would listen for a moment till the hurry-scurry had
clattered by, and then exclaim, "Ay, there goes Brom
Bones and his gang!" The neighbors looked upon him
30 with a mixture of awe, admiration, and good will; and
when any madcap prank or rustic brawl occurred in
the vicinity, always shook their heads, and warranted
Brom Bones was at the bottom of it.

This rantipole hero had for some time singled out the
35 blooming Katrina for the object of his uncouth gallan-

tries, and though his amorous toyings were something
like the gentle caresses and endearments of a bear, yet it
was whispered that she did not altogether discourage his
hopes. Certain it is, his advances were signals for rival
5 candidates to retire, who felt no inclination to cross a lion
in his amours; insomuch, that when his horse was seen
tied to Van Tassel's paling, on a Sunday night, a sure
sign that his master was courting, or, as it is termed,
"sparking," within, all other suitors passed by in despair,
10 and carried the war into other quarters.

Such was the formidable rival with whom Ichabod
Crane had to contend, and considering all things, a
stouter man than he would have shrunk from the competition, and a wiser man would have despaired. He had,
15 however, a happy mixture of pliability and perseverance
in his nature; he was in form and spirit like a supple-
jack—yielding but tough; though he bent, he never broke;
and though he bowed beneath the slightest pressure, yet,
the moment it was away—jerk! he was as erect, and
20 carried his head as high as ever.

To have taken the field openly against his rival
would have been madness; for he was not a man to be
thwarted in his amours, any more than that stormy lover,
Achilles. Ichabod, therefore, made his advances in a
25 quiet and gently-insinuating manner. Under cover of
his character of singing-master, he made frequent visits
at the farmhouse; not that he had anything to apprehend
from the meddlesome interference of parents, which is
so often a stumbling-block in the path of lovers. Balt
30 Van Tassel was an easy, indulgent soul; he loved his
daughter better even than his pipe, and, like a reasonable
man and an excellent father, let her have her way in
everything. His notable little wife, too, had enough to
do to attend to her housekeeping and manage her poultry,
35 for, as she sagely observed, ducks and geese are foolish

things, and must be looked after, but girls can take care
of themselves. Thus, while the busy dame bustled about
the house, or plied her spinning-wheel at one end of the
piazza, honest Balt would sit smoking his evening pipe
5 at the other, watching the achievements of a little wooden
warrior, who, armed with a sword in each hand, was most
valiantly fighting the wind on the pinnacle of the barn.
In the meantime, Ichabod would carry on his suit with
the daughter by the side of the spring under the great
10 elm, or sauntering along in the twilight, that hour so
favorable to the lover's eloquence.

I profess not to know how women's hearts are wooed
and won. To me they have always been matters of riddle
and admiration. Some seem to have but one vulnerable
15 point, or door of access; while others have a thousand
avenues, and may be captured in a thousand different
ways. It is a great triumph of skill to gain the former, but
a still greater proof of generalship to maintain possession
of the latter, for a man must battle for his fortress at every
20 door and window. He who wins a thousand common
hearts is therefore entitled to some renown; but he who
keeps undisputed sway over the heart of a coquette, is indeed a hero. Certain it is, this was not the case with the
redoubtable Brom Bones; and from the moment Ichabod
25 Crane made his advances, the interests of the former evidently declined; his horse was no longer seen tied at the
palings on Sunday nights, and a deadly feud gradually
arose between him and the preceptor of Sleepy Hollow.

Brom, who had a degree of rough chivalry in his
30 nature, would fain have carried matters to open warfare,
and have settled their pretensions to the lady, according
to the mode of those most concise and simple reasoners,
the knights-errant of yore—by single combat; but Ichabod
was too conscious of the superior might of his adversary
35 to enter the lists against him: he had overheard the boast

of Bones, that he would "double the schoolmaster up, and
lay him on a shelf of his own schoolhouse"; and he was
too wary to give him an opportunity. There was something extremely provoking in this obstinately pacific sys-
5 tem; it left Brom no alternative but to draw upon the
funds of rustic waggery in his disposition, and to play off
boorish practical jokes upon his rival. Ichabod became
the object of whimsical persecution to Bones, and his gang
of rough riders. They harried his hitherto peaceful do-
10 mains; smoked out his singing school, by stopping up the
chimney; broke into the schoolhouse at night, in spite of
its formidable fastenings of withe and window stakes, and
turned everything topsy-turvy: so that the poor schoolmaster began to think all the witches in the country held
15 their meetings there. But what was still more annoying,
Brom took all opportunities of turning him into ridicule
in presence of his mistress, and had a scoundrel dog whom
he taught to whine in a most ludicrous manner, and introduced as a rival of Ichabod's to instruct her in psalmody.
20   In this way matters went on for some time, without
producing any material effect on the relative situation
of the contending powers. On a fine autumnal afternoon,
Ichabod, in pensive mood, sat enthroned on the lofty stool
whence he usually watched all the concerns of his little
25 literary realm. In his hand he swayed a ferule, that
scepter of despotic power; the birch of justice re-
posed on three nails, behind the throne, a constant terror
to evil-doers; while on the desk before him might be seen
sundry contraband articles and prohibited weapons, de-
30 tected upon the persons of idle urchins; such as half-
munched apples, pop-guns, whirligigs, fly-cages, and whole
legions of rampant little paper game-cocks. Apparently
there had been some appalling act of justice recently inflicted, for his scholars were all busily intent upon their
35 books, or slyly whispering behind them with one eye kept

upon the master; and a kind of buzzing stillness reigned throughout the schoolroom. It was suddenly interrupted by the appearance of a negro, in tow-cloth jacket and trowsers, a round-crowned fragment of a hat, like
5 the cap of Mercury, and mounted on the back of a ragged, wild, half-broken colt, which he managed with a rope by way of halter. He came clattering up to the school door with an invitation to Ichabod to attend a merrymaking or "quilting frolic," to be held that evening at Mynheer
10 Van Tassel's; and having delivered his message with that air of importance, and effort at fine language, which a negro is apt to display on petty embassies of the kind, he dashed over the brook, and was seen scampering away up the hollow, full of the importance and hurry of his
15 mission.

All was now bustle and hubbub in the late quiet schoolroom. The scholars were hurried through their lessons, without stopping at trifles; those who were nimble skipped over half with impunity, and those who were
20 tardy, had a smart application now and then in the rear, to quicken their speed, or help them over a tall word. Books were flung aside without being put away on the shelves, inkstands were overturned, benches thrown down, and the whole school was turned loose an hour
25 before the usual time, bursting forth like a legion of young imps, yelping and racketing about the green, in joy at their early emancipation.

The gallant Ichabod now spent at least an extra half-hour at his toilet, brushing and furbishing up his best,
30 and indeed only suit of rusty black, and arranging his locks by a bit of broken looking-glass, that hung up in the schoolhouse. That he might make his appearance before his mistress in the true style of a cavalier, he borrowed a horse from the farmer with whom he was domi-
35 ciliated, a choleric old Dutchman, of the name of Hans

Van Ripper, and, thus gallantly mounted, issued forth,
like a knight-errant in quest of adventures. But it is
meet I should, in the true spirit of romantic story, give
some account of the looks and equipments of my hero
5 and his steed. The animal he bestrode was a broken-
down plough-horse, that had outlived almost everything
but his viciousness. He was gaunt and shagged, with
a ewe neck and a head like a hammer; his rusty mane
and tail were tangled and knotted with burrs; one eye
10 had lost its pupil, and was glaring and spectral; but the
other had the gleam of a genuine devil in it. Still he must
have had fire and mettle in his day, if we may judge from
the name he bore of Gunpowder. He had, in fact, been
a favorite steed of his master's, the choleric Van Ripper,
15 who was a furious rider, and had infused, very probably,
some of his own spirit into the animal; for, old and
broken-down as he looked, there was more of the lurking
devil in him than in any young filly in the country.

Ichabod was a suitable figure for such a steed. He
20 rode with short stirrups, which brought his knees nearly
up to the pommel of the saddle; his sharp elbows stuck
out like grasshoppers'; he carried his whip perpendicu-
larly in his hand, like a scepter, and, as the horse jogged
on, the motion of his arms was not unlike the flapping of
25 a pair of wings. A small wool hat rested on the top of
his nose, for so his scanty strip of forehead might be called;
and the skirts of his black coat fluttered out almost to
the horse's tail. Such was the appearance of Ichabod
and his steed as they shambled out of the gate of Hans
30 Van Ripper, and it was altogether such an apparition as
is seldom to be met with in broad daylight.

It was, as I have said, a fine autumnal day; the sky
was clear and serene, and nature wore that rich and
golden livery which we always associate with the idea
35 of abundance. The forests had put on their sober brown

and yellow, while some trees of the tenderer kind had
been nipped by the frosts into brilliant dyes of orange,
purple, and scarlet. Streaming files of wild ducks began
to make their appearance high in the air; the bark of the
5 squirrel might be heard from the groves of beech and
hickory nuts, and the pensive whistle of the quail at in-
tervals from the neighboring stubble field.

The small birds were taking their farewell banquets.
In the fullness of their revelry, they fluttered, chirping
10 and frolicing, from bush to bush, and tree to tree, capricious
from the very profusion and variety around them.
There was the honest cock-robin, the favorite game of
stripling sportsmen, with its loud querulous note, and
the twittering blackbirds flying in sable clouds; and the
15 golden-winged woodpecker, with his crimson crest, his
broad black gorget, and splendid plumage; and the cedar-
bird, with its red-tipt wings and yellow-tipt tail, and
its little monteiro cap of feathers; and the blue jay,
that noisy coxcomb, in his gay light-blue coat and white
20 underclothes, screaming and chattering, nodding and
bobbing and bowing, and pretending to be on good terms
with every songster of the grove.

As Ichabod jogged slowly on his way, his eye, ever open
to every symptom of culinary abundance, ranged with
25 delight over the treasures of jolly autumn. On all sides
he beheld vast stores of apples; some hanging in oppressive opulence on the trees; some gathered into baskets
and barrels for the market; others heaped up in rich
piles for the cider-press. Farther on he beheld great
30 fields of Indian corn, with its golden ears peeping from
their leafy coverts, and holding out the promise of cakes
and hasty-pudding; and the yellow pumpkins lying beneath them turning up their fair round bellies to the
sun, and giving ample prospect of the most luxurious
35 of pies; and anon he passed fragrant buckwheat fields,

breathing the odor of the beehive, and as he beheld them,
soft anticipation stole over his mind of dainty slap-jacks,
well buttered, and garnished with honey or treacle, by
the delicate little dimpled hand of Katrina Van Tassel.
5   Thus feeding his mind with many sweet thoughts and
"sugared suppositions," he journeyed along the sides of
a range of hills which look out upon some of the goodliest
scenes of the mighty Hudson. The sun gradually
wheeled his broad disc down in the west. The wide
10 bosom of the Tappan Zee lay motionless and glassy, excepting that here and there a gentle undulation waved
and prolonged the blue shadow of the distant mountain.
A few amber clouds floated in the sky, without a breath of
air to move them. The horizon was of a fine golden tint,
15 changing gradually into a pure apple green, and from
that into the deep blue of the mid-heaven. A slanting
ray lingered on the woody crests of the precipices that
overhung some parts of the river, giving greater depth
to the dark gray and purple of their rocky sides. A sloop
20 was loitering in the distance, dropping slowly down with
the tide, her sail hanging uselessly against the mast; and
as the reflection of the sky gleamed along the still water,
it seemed as if the vessel was suspended in the air.

It was toward evening that Ichabod arrived at the
25 castle of the Heer Van Tassel, which he found thronged
with the pride and flower of the adjacent country—old
farmers, a spare leathern-faced race, in homespun coats
and breeches, blue stockings, huge shoes, and magnificent
pewter buckles; their brisk, withered little dames, in
30 close-crimped caps, long-waisted gowns, homespun petti-
coats, with scissors and pin-cushions, and gay calico
pockets hanging on the outside; buxom lasses, almost as
antiquated as their mothers, excepting where a straw hat,
a fine ribbon, or perhaps a white frock, gave symptoms
35 of city innovation; the sons, in short square-skirted

coats with rows of stupendous brass buttons, and their
hair generally queued in the fashion of the times, especially if they could procure an eelskin for the purpose, it
being esteemed throughout the country, as a potent
5 nourisher and strengthener of the hair.

Brom Bones, however, was the hero of the scene,
having come to the gathering on his favorite steed Daredevil, a creature like himself, full of mettle and mischief,
and which no one but himself could manage. He was,
10 in fact, noted for preferring vicious animals, given to all
kinds of tricks, which kept the rider in constant risk of
his neck, for he held a tractable well-broken horse as un-
worthy of a lad of spirit.

Fain would I pause to dwell upon the world of charms
15 that burst upon the enraptured gaze of my hero, as he
entered the state parlor of Van Tassel's mansion. Not
those of the bevy of buxom lasses, with their luxurious
display of red and white; but the ample charms of a
genuine Dutch country tea table, in the sumptuous time
20 of autumn. Such heaped-up platters of cakes of various
and almost indescribable kinds, known only to the experienced Dutch housewives! There was the doughty
doughnut, the tender oly-koek, and the crisp and crum-
bling cruller; sweet cakes and short cakes, ginger cakes
25 and honey cakes, and the whole family of cakes. And
then there were apple pies and peach pies and pumpkin
pies; besides slices of ham and smoked beef; and moreover delectable dishes of preserved plums, and peaches,
and pears, and quinces; not to mention broiled shad and
30 roasted chickens; together with bowls of milk and cream,
all mingled higgledy-piggledy, pretty much as I have enu-
merated them, with the motherly teapot sending up its
clouds of vapor from the midst—Heaven bless the
mark! I want breath and time to discuss this banquet
35 as it deserves, and am too eager to get on with my

story. Happily, Ichabod Crane was not in so great
a hurry as his historian, but did ample justice to every
dainty.

He was a kind and thankful creature, whose heart
5 dilated in proportion as his skin was filled with good cheer;
and whose spirits rose with eating, as some men's do
with drink. He could not help, too, rolling his large eyes
round him as he ate, and chuckling with the possibility
that he might one day be lord of all this scene of almost
10 unimaginable luxury and splendor. Then, he thought,
how soon he'd turn his back upon the old schoolhouse;
snap his fingers in the face of Hans Van Ripper, and every
other niggardly patron, and kick any itinerant pedagogue
out of doors that should dare call him comrade!
15   Old Baltus Van Tassel moved about among his guests
with a face dilated with content and good humor, round
and jolly as the harvest moon. His hospitable attentions
were brief, but expressive, being confined to a shake of
the hand, a slap on the shoulder, a loud laugh, and a
20 pressing invitation to "fall to, and help themselves."

And now the sound of the music from the common
room, or hall, summoned to the dance. The musician
was an old gray-headed negro, who had been the itinerant
orchestra of the neighborhood for more than half a cen-
25 tury. His instrument was as old and battered as himself. The greater part of the time he scraped away on
two or three strings, accompanying every movement of
the bow with a motion of the head; bowing almost to the
ground, and stamping with his foot whenever a fresh
30 couple were to start.

Ichabod prided himself upon his dancing as much as
upon his vocal powers. Not a limb, not a fiber about
him was idle; and to have seen his loosely hung frame in
full motion, and clattering about the room, you would
35 have thought St. Vitus himself, that blessed patron of

the dance, was figuring before you in person. He was
the admiration of all the negroes; who, having gathered,
of all ages and sizes, from the farm and the neighborhood,
stood forming a pyramid of shining black faces at every
5 door and window, gazing with delight at the scene, rolling
their white eye-balls, and showing grinning rows of ivory
from ear to ear. How could the flogger of urchins be
otherwise than animated and joyous? the lady of his
heart was his partner in the dance, and smiling graciously
10 in reply to all his amorous oglings; while Brom Bones,
sorely smitten with love and jealousy, sat brooding by
himself in one corner.

When the dance was at an end, Ichabod was attracted
to a knot of the sager folks, who, with old Van Tassel, sat
15 smoking at one end of the piazza, gossiping over former
times, and drawling out long stories about the war.

This neighborhood, at the time of which I am speaking, was one of those highly favored places which abound
with chronicle and great men. The British and American
20 line had run near it during the war; it had, therefore, been
the scene of marauding, and infested with refugees, cow-
boys, and all kinds of border chivalry. Just sufficient
time had elapsed to enable each story-teller to dress up
his tale with a little becoming fiction, and, in the indis-
25 tinctness of his recollection, to make himself the hero of
every exploit.

There was the story of Doffue Martling, a large, blue-
bearded Dutchman, who had nearly taken a British
frigate with an old iron nine-pounder from a mud breast-
30 work, only that his gun burst at the sixth discharge.
And there was an old gentleman who shall be nameless,
being too rich a mynheer to be lightly mentioned, who,
in the battle of White Plains, being an excellent master
of defense, parried a musket ball with a small sword, in-
35 somuch that he absolutely felt it whiz round the blade,

and glance off at the hilt: in proof of which he was ready
at any time to show the sword, with the hilt a little bent.
There were several more that had been equally great in
the field, not one of whom but was persuaded that he
5 had a considerable hand in bringing the war to a happy
termination.

But all these were nothing to the tales of ghosts and
apparitions that succeeded. The neighborhood is rich in
legendary treasures of the kind. Local tales and super-
10 stitions thrive best in these sheltered long-settled re-
treats; but are trampled under foot by the shifting throng
that forms the population of most of our country places.
Besides, there is no encouragement for ghosts in most of
our villages, for they have scarcely had time to finish
15 their first nap, and turn themselves in their graves, before
their surviving friends have traveled away from the
neighborhood; so that when they turn out at night to
walk their rounds, thay have no acquaintance left to call
upon. This is perhaps the reason why we so seldom hear
20 of ghosts except in our long-established Dutch communi-
ties.

The immediate cause, however, of the prevalence of
supernatural stories in these parts, was doubtless owing
to the vicinity of Sleepy Hollow. There was a contagion
25 in the very air that blew from that haunted region; it
breathed forth an atmosphere of dreams and fancies in-
fecting all the land. Several of the Sleepy Hollow people
were present at Van Tassel's, and, as usual, were doling˙
out their wild and wonderful legends. Many dismal
30 tales were told about funeral trains and mourning cries
and wailings heard and seen about the great tree where
the unfortunate Major André was taken, and which
stood in the neighborhood. Some mention was made also
of the woman in white, that haunted the dark glen at
35 Ravenrock, and was often heard to shriek on winter

nights before a storm, having perished there in the snow. The chief part of the stories, however, turned upon the favorite specter of Sleepy Hollow, the Headless Horseman, who had been heard several times of late, patroling 5 the country; and, it was said, tethered his horse nightly among the graves in the churchyard.

The sequestered situation of this church seems always to have made it a favorite haunt of troubled spirits. It stands on a knoll, surrounded by locust trees and lofty 10 elms, from among which its decent, white-washed walls shine modestly forth, like Christian purity, beaming through the shades of retirement. A gentle slope descends from it to a silver sheet of water, bordered by high trees, between which, peeps may be caught at the blue 15 hills of the Hudson. To look upon its grass-grown yard, where the sunbeams seem to sleep so quietly, one would think that there at least the dead might rest in peace. On one side of the church extends a wide woody dell, along which raves a large brook among broken rocks and 20 trunks of fallen trees. Over a deep black part of the stream, not far from the church, was formerly thrown a wooden bridge; the road that led to it, and the bridge itself, were thickly shaded by overhanging trees, which cast a gloom about it, even in the daytime; but occasioned 25 a fearful darkness at night. This was one of the favorite haunts of the Headless Horseman and the place where he was most frequently encountered. The tale was told of old Brouwer, a most heretical disbeliever in ghosts, how he met the horseman returning from his foray into Sleepy 30 Hollow, and was obliged to get up behind him; how they galloped over bush and brake, over hill and swamp, until they reached the bridge, when the horseman suddenly turned into a skeleton, threw old Brouwer into the brook, and sprang away over the tree-tops with a clap of thunder. 35 This story was immediately matched by a thrice mar-

velous adventure of Brom Bones, who made light of the
Galloping Hessian as an arrant jockey. He affirmed that,
on returning one night from the neighboring village of
Sing Sing, he had been overtaken by this midnight
5 trooper; that he had offered to race with him for a bowl of
punch, and should have won it too, for Daredevil beat
the goblin horse all hollow; but just as they came to the
church bridge, the Hessian bolted, and vanished in a
flash of fire.

10   All these tales, told in that drowsy undertone with
which men talk in the dark, the countenances of the lis-
teners only now and then receiving a casual gleam from
the glare of a pipe, sank deep in the mind of Ichabod.
He repaid them in kind with large extracts from his in-
15 valuable author, Cotton Mather, and added many marvelous events that had taken place in his native state of
Connecticut, and fearful sights which he had seen in his
nightly walks about Sleepy Hollow.

The revel now gradually broke up.   The old farmers
20 gathered together their families in their wagons, and were
heard for some time rattling along the hollow roads, and
over the distant hills. Some of the damsels mounted
on pillions behind their favorite swains, and their light-
hearted laughter, mingling with the clatter of hoofs,
25 echoed along the silent woodlands, sounding fainter and
fainter, until they gradually died away—and the late
scene of noise and frolic was all silent and deserted.
Ichabod only lingered behind, according to the custom
of country lovers, to have a "tête-à-tête" with the heiress,
30 fully convinced that he was now on the high road to success.   What passed at this interview I will not pretend to
say, for I do not know. Something, however, I fear me, must
have gone wrong, for he certainly sallied forth, after no
very great interval, with an air quite desolate and chap-
35 fallen—oh, these women! these women! Could that girl

have been playing off any of her coquettish tricks?—Was
her encouragement of the poor pedagogue all a mere sham
to secure her conquest of his rival?—Heaven only knows,
not I!—Let it suffice to say, Ichabod stole forth with the
5 air of one who had been sacking a henroost, rather than
a fair lady's heart. Without looking to the right or left
to notice the scene of rural wealth, on which he had so
often gloated, he went straight to the stable, and with
several hearty cuffs and kicks, roused his steed most un-
10 courteously from the comfortable quarters in which he
was soundly sleeping, dreaming of mountains of corn and
oats, and whole valleys of timothy and clover.

It was the very witching time of night that Ichabod,
heavy-hearted and crest-fallen, pursued his travel home-
15 wards, along the sides of the lofty hills which rise above
Tarry Town, and which he had traversed so cheerily in
the afternoon. The hour was as dismal as himself. Far
below him, the Tappan Zee spread its dusky and indis-
tinct waste of waters, with here and there the tall mast of
20 a sloop, riding quietly at anchor under the land. In the
dead hush of midnight, he could even hear the barking of
the watchdog from the opposite shore of the Hudson; but
it was so vague and faint as only to give an idea of his
distance from this faithful companion of man. Now and
25 then, too, the long-drawn crowing of a cock accidently
awakened, would sound far, far off, from some farmhouse
away among the hills—but it was like a dreaming sound in
his ear. No signs of life occurred near him, but occasionally the melancholy chirp of a cricket, or perhaps the gut-
30 tural twang of a bullfrog from a neighboring marsh, as if
sleeping uncomfortably, and turning suddenly in his bed.

All the stories of ghosts and goblins that he had heard
in the afternoon, now came crowding upon his recollection.
The night grew darker and darker; the stars seemed to
35 sink deeper in the sky, and driving clouds occasionally hid

them from his sight. He had never felt so lonely and
dismal. He was, moreover, approaching the very place
where many of the scenes of the ghost stories had been
laid. In the center of the road stood an enormous tulip-
5 tree, which towered like a giant above all the other trees
of the neighborhood, and formed a kind of landmark. Its
limbs were gnarled and fantastic, large enough to form
trunks for ordinary trees, twisting down almost to the
earth, and rising again into the air. It was connected
10 with the tragical story of the unfortunate André, who had
been taken prisoner hard by; and was universally known
by the name of Major André's tree. The common people
regarded it with a mixture of respect and superstition,
partly out of sympathy for the fate of its ill-starred name-
15 sake, and partly from the tales of strange sights and dole-
ful lamentations told concerning it.

As Ichabod approached this fearful tree he began to
whistle: he thought his whistle was answered; it was but
a blast sweeping sharply through the dry branches. As
20 he approached a little nearer, he thought he saw something white hanging in the midst of the tree; he paused,
and ceased whistling; but on looking more narrowly, perceived that it was a place where the tree had been
scathed by lightning, and the white wood laid bare.
25 Suddenly he heard a groan—his teeth chattered, his knees
smote against the saddle; it was but the rubbing of one
huge bough upon another, as they were swayed about by
the breeze. He passed the tree in safety, but new perils
lay before him.

30 About two hundred yards from the tree a small brook
crossed the road, and ran into a marshy and thickly
wooded glen, known by the name of Wiley's Swamp. A
few rough logs, laid side by side, served for a bridge over
this stream. On that side of the road where the brook
35 entered the wood, a group of oaks and chestnuts, matted

thick with wild grapevines, threw a cavernous gloom over
it. To pass this bridge was the severest trial. It was at
this identical spot that the unfortunate André was captured, and under the covert of those chestnuts and vines
5 were the sturdy yeomen concealed who surprised him.
This has ever since been considered a haunted stream,
and fearful are the feelings of a schoolboy who has to
pass it alone after dark.

As he approached the stream his heart began to
10 thump; he summoned up, however, all his resolution,
gave his horse half a score of kicks in the ribs and attempted to dash briskly across the bridge; but instead of
starting forward, the perverse old animal made a lateral
movement, and ran broadside against the fence. Ichabod,
15 whose fears increased with the delay, jerked the reins on
the other side, and kicked lustily with the contrary foot:
it was all in vain; his steed started, it is true, but it was
only to plunge to the opposite side of the road into a
thicket of brambles and alder bushes. The schoolmaster
20 now bestowed both whip and heel upon the starveling
ribs of old Gunpowder, who dashed forward, snuffling and
snorting, but came to a stand just by the bridge, with a
suddenness that had nearly sent his rider sprawling over
his head. Just at this moment a plashy tramp by the
25 side of the bridge caught the sensitive ear of Ichabod.
In the dark shadow of the grove, on the margin of the
brook, he beheld something huge, misshapen, black and
towering. It stirred not, but seemed gathered up in the
gloom like some gigantic monster ready to spring upon
30 the traveler.

The hair of the affrighted pedagogue rose upon his
head with terror. What was to be done? To turn and
fly was now too late; and besides, what chance was there
of escaping ghost or goblin, if such it was, which could
35 ride upon the wings of the wind? Summoning up, there-

fore, a show of courage, he demanded in stammering ac-
cents—"Who are you?" He received no reply. He repeated his demand in a still more agitated voice. Still
there was no answer. Once more he cudgeled the sides
5 of the inflexible Gunpowder, and shutting his eyes, broke
forth with involuntary fervor into a psalm tune. Just
then the shadowy object of alarm put itself in motion,
and, with a scramble and a bound, stood at once in the
middle of the road. Though the night was dark and dis-
10 mal, yet the form of the unknown might now in some
degree be ascertained. He appeared to be a horseman of
large dimensions, and mounted on a black horse of powerful frame. He made no offer of molestation or socia-
bility, but kept aloof on one side of the road, jogging
15 along on the blind side of old Gunpowder, who had now
got over his fright and waywardness.

Ichabod, who had no relish for this strange midnight
companion, and bethought himself of the adventure of
Brom Bones with the Galloping Hessian, now quickened
20 his steed, in hopes of leaving him behind. The stranger,
however, quickened his horse to an equal pace. Ichabod
pulled up, and fell into a walk, thinking to lag behind—
the other did the same. His heart began to sink within
him; he endeavored to resume his psalm tune, but his
25 parched tongue clove to the roof of his mouth and he
could not utter a stave. There was something in the
moody and dogged silence of this pertinacious companion,
that was mysterious and appalling. It was soon fearfully
accounted for. On mounting a rising ground, which
30 brought the figure of his fellow-traveler in relief against
the sky, gigantic in height, and muffled in a cloak, Ichabod was horror-struck, on perceiving that he was headless!—but his horror was still more increased, on
observing that the head, which should have rested on
35 his shoulders, was carried before him on the pommel of

his saddle: his terror rose to desperation; he rained a
shower of kicks and blows upon Gunpowder, hoping, by
a sudden movement, to give his companion the slip—but
the specter started full jump with him. Away then they
5 dashed, through thick and thin; stones flying, and sparks
flashing at every bound. Ichabod's flimsy garments fluttered in the air, as he stretched his long lank body
away over his horse's head, in the eagerness of his flight.

They had now reached the road which turns off to
10 Sleepy Hollow; but Gunpowder, who seemed possessed
with a demon, instead of keeping up it, made an opposite
turn and plunged headlong down hill to the left. This
road leads through a sandy hollow shaded by trees for
about a quarter of a mile, where it crosses the bridge
15 famous in goblin story, and just beyond swells the green
knoll on which stands the whitewashed church.

As yet the panic of the steed had given his unskillful
rider an apparent advantage in the chase; but just as he
had got half way through the hollow, the girths of the
20 saddle gave way, and he felt it slipping from under him.
He seized it by the pommel, and endeavored to hold it
firm, but in vain; and had just time to save himself by
clasping old Gunpowder round the neck, when the saddle
fell to the earth, and he heard it trampled under foot by
25 his pursuer. For a moment the terror of Hans Van
Ripper's wrath passed across his mind—for it was his Sunday saddle; but this was no time for petty fears; the goblin was hard on his haunches; and (unskillful rider that
he was!) he had much ado to maintain his seat; sometimes
30 slipping on one side, sometimes on another, and sometimes
jolted on the high ridge of his horse's back bone, with a
violence that he verily feared would cleave him asunder.

An opening in the trees now cheered him with the
hopes that the church bridge was at hand. The waver-
35 ing reflection of a silver star in the bosom of the brook

told him that he was not mistaken. He saw the walls of
the church dimly glaring under the trees beyond. He
recollected the place where Brom Bones' ghostly competitor had disappeared. "If I can but reach that
5 bridge," thought Ichabod, "I am safe." Just then he
heard the black steed panting and blowing close behind
him; he even fancied that he felt his hot breath. Another convulsive kick in the ribs, and old Gunpowder
sprang upon the bridge; he thundered over the resounding
10 planks; he gained the opposite side, and now Ichabod
cast a look behind to see if his pursuer should vanish,
according to rule, in a flash of fire and brimstone. Just
then he saw the goblin rising in his stirrups, and in the
very act of hurling his head at him. Ichabod endeavored
15 to dodge the horrible missile, but too late. It encountered his cranium with a tremendous crash—he was tumbled headlong into the dust, and Gunpowder, the black
steed, and the goblin rider, passed by like a whirlwind.

The next morning the old horse was found without his
20 saddle, and with the bridle under his feet, soberly cropping
the grass at his master's gate. Ichabod did not make his
appearance at breakfast—dinner hour came, but no Ichabod. The boys assembled at the schoolhouse and
strolled idly about the banks of the brook; but no school-
25 master. Hans Van Ripper now began to feel some un-
easiness about the fate of poor Ichabod and his saddle.
An inquiry was set on foot, and after diligent investigation they came upon his traces. In one part of the road
leading to the church was found the saddle trampled in
30 the dirt; the tracks of horses' hoofs deeply dented in the
road, and evidently at furious speed, were traced to the
bridge, beyond which, on the bank of a broad part of the
brook, where the water ran deep and black, was found
the hat of the unfortunate Ichabod, and close beside it a
35 shattered pumpkin.

The brook was searched, but the body of the school-master was not to be discovered. Hans Van Ripper, as executor of his estate, examined the bundle which contained all his worldly effects. They consisted of two
5 shirts and a half; two stocks for the neck; a pair or two of worsted stockings; an old pair of corduroy small-clothes; a rusty razor; a book of psalm tunes, full of dog's ears; and a broken pitch pipe. As to the books and furniture of the schoolhouse they belonged to the com-
10 munity, excepting Cotton Mather's "History of Witch-craft," a New England Almanac, and a book of dreams and fortune-telling; in which last was a sheet of foolscap much scribbled and blotted in several fruitless attempts to make a copy of verses in honor of the heiress of Van
15 Tassel. These magic books and the poetic scrawl were forthwith consigned to the flames by Hans Van Ripper; who from that time forward determined to send his children no more to school; observing that he never knew any good come of this same reading and writing. What-
20 ever money the schoolmaster possessed, and he had received his quarter's pay but a day or two before, he must have had about his person at the time of his disappearance.

The mysterious event caused much speculation at the
25 church on the following Sunday. Knots of gazers and gossips were collected in the churchyard, at the bridge, and at the spot where the hat and pumpkin had been found. The stories of Brouwer, of Bones, and a whole budget of others, were called to mind; and when they had
30 diligently considered them all, and compared them with the symptoms of the present case, they shook their heads, and came to the conclusion that Ichabod had been carried off by the Galloping Hessian. As he was a bachelor, and in nobody's debt, nobody troubled his head any more
35 about him. The school was removed to a different quarter

of the Hollow and another pedagogue reigned in his stead.

It is true, an old farmer, who had been down to New York on a visit several years after, and from whom this 5 account of the ghostly adventure was received, brought home the intelligence that Ichabod Crane was still alive; that he had left the neighborhood, partly through fear of the goblin and Hans Van Ripper, and partly in mortification at having been suddenly dismissed by the heiress; 10 that he had changed his quarters to a distant part of the country; had kept school and studied law at the same time; had been admitted to the bar; turned politician; electioneered; written for the newspapers, and finally had been made a Justice of the Ten Pound Court. Brom 15 Bones too, who shortly after his rival's disappearance conducted the blooming Katrina in triumph to the altar, was observed to look exceedingly knowing whenever the story of Ichabod was related, and always burst into a hearty laugh at the mention of the pumpkin; which led 20 some to suspect that he knew more about the matter than he chose to tell.

The old country wives, however, who are the best judges of these matters, maintain to this day that Ichabod was spirited away by supernatural means; and it is 25 a favorite story often told about the neighborhood round the winter evening fire. The bridge became more than ever an object of superstitious awe, and that may be the reason why the road has been altered of late years, so as to approach the church by the border of the mill pond. 30 The schoolhouse being deserted, soon fell to decay, and was reported to be haunted by the ghost of the unfortunate pedagogue, and the plough boy, loitering homeward of a still summer evening, has often fancied his voice at a distance, chanting a melancholy psalm tune among the 35 tranquil solitudes of Sleepy Hollow.

NOTES AND SUGGESTIONS

In writings classed as narration, the action usually begins promptly and moves along to a climax which, as a rule, is near the end of the story. In regard to the action of the piece, the narrator may leave himself open to criticism in three ways: first, he may be slow in beginning it; second, he may turn aside from his story to tell of other matters; third; he may be slow in ending it, i.e., he may tag on unnecessary material after the climax has been reached.

1. Where does the action of this story begin?
2. Specify the topics touched upon before Irving commences the story proper.
3. a. In the opening description of the scene of the story, what characteristics are made prominent?
   b. What bearing has this description on the story that follows?
4. What characters does the author describe?
5. a. Who is the chief character of the tale?
   b. Mention some of the traits of character brought out in this person.
   c. Why does the author make him so contemptible?
6. a. Name the important traits of character portrayed in the other two persons described.
   b. Show the bearing of those characteristics on the plot of the piece.
7. a. In the paragraph beginning on page 4, line 22, pick out the metaphors and similes used.
   b. What is the effect of these figures?
8. Trace briefly the action of the story.
9. a. Describe in your own words the schoolhouse at Sleepy Hollow.
   b. Point out the elements of humor in Irving's description of it.
10. Page 5, line 20, why does the author speak of the tree as a *formidable* birch?
11. In the paragraph beginning on page 29, line 13, the author wishes us to feel the loneliness of the scene; how does he gain the desired effect?
12. Point out the paragraph that contains the climax of the story.
13. Why are the paragraphs that follow, necessary?
14. Summarize the author's method of telling this story, in regard to the action of it and the humor of it.

Explanatory Notes

Page 3, line 6—"nightmare, with her whole ninefold": the nightmare's ninefold are her nine imps or attendant spirits; the quotation is from King Lear, Act III, sc. IV (Shakespeare).

Page 8, line 13—"gazette"—a newspaper, a printed sheet published periodically.

Page 8, line 18—"Cotton Mather"—a Puritan preacher and writer, born in 1663 and died in 1728. He was the author of many books, including "Memorable Providences relating to Witchcraft and Possession." He was active in the persecution of the so-called witches of Salem.

Page 9, line 10—"witch's token"—this was supposed to be some visible sign by which a person knew he was under the power of a witch.

Page 11, line 4—"Saardam"—a small town in Holland.

Page 15, line 6—"Tartar"—the Tartars were the inhabitants of Tartary, at one time an important province in Asia. They were noted for their horsemanship.

Page 15, line 26—"Don Cossacks" —a branch of the Cossack people, inhabiting the country near the River Don. They were daring and splendid horsemen.

Page 15, line 34—"rantipole hero"; wild, reckless; a madcap. A nickname given to Emperor Napoleon III.

Page 19, line 5—"Mercury"— in Roman mythology, the messenger of the gods. Usually represented with wings on his heels that he might travel swiftly through space.

Page 24, line 35—"St. Vitus"— sometimes called the patron saint of the dance. He was supposed to have control over the nervous and hysterical affections.

Page 28, line 29—"tête-à-tête"— a confidential talk. Literally translated, it means, "head-to-head."

Page 29, line 13—"the very witching time of night"—expression used by Shakespeare in Hamlet, Act III, sc. II.

Page 36, line 14—"Ten Pound Court"—a court in which cases, involving not more than ten pounds (about $50), were tried.

Suggestions for Home Reading of Books from the Public Library or Class Library

Dickens' "The Signal Man"—a story in which the mysterious is treated of, but from a very different point of view from that employed by Irving in "The Legend of Sleepy Hollow."

Twain's "A Dog's Tale"—an animal story of rare pathos.

THE PURLOINED LETTER

BY EDGAR ALLAN POE

EDGAR ALLAN POE was born in Boston in 1809 and died in Baltimore in 1849. He is noted as a poet and a writer of tales. His life was a most unhappy one. Throughout its course, his lack of self-control and of any moral sense was the cause of misery and sorrow to himself and to all who loved him. Poe was left without father or mother when he was two years old and was adopted by a Mr. John Allan who provided for his education. Poe antagonized this kind friend by his ingratitude and his repeated follies. When Mr. Allan refused to aid him further, Poe turned to literary work as a means of livelihood. He did a great deal of newspaper and magazine work. Most of his tales appeared first in periodicals. With the publication of the poem, "The Raven," in 1845, Poe reached the summit of his success.

"The Purloined Letter" is one of Poe's detective stories. Dupin, the solver of mysteries, appears in the other two tales of this type, "The Murders of Rue Morgue" and "The Mystery of Marie Roget." Poe's method of constructing these stories has been imitated by many of the present-day writers of stories of this kind.

AT Paris, just after dark one gusty evening in the autumn of 18—, I was enjoying the twofold luxury of meditation and a meerschaum, in company with my friend, C. Auguste Dupin, in his little back library, or book-closet,
5 No. 33 Rue Dunot. For one hour at least we had maintained a profound silence; while each, to the casual observer, might have seemed intently and exclusively occupied with the curling eddies of smoke that oppressed the atmosphere of the chamber. For myself, however, I was
10 mentally discussing certain topics which had formed matter of conversation between us at an earlier period of the evening; I mean the affair of the Rue Morgue and the mystery attending the murder of Marie Roget. I looked upon it, therefore, as something of a coincidence, when the

door of our apartment was thrown open and admitted our old acquaintance, Monsieur G——, the Prefect of the Parisian police.

We gave him a hearty welcome; for there was nearly
5 half as much of the entertaining as of the contemptible about the man, and we had not seen him for several years. We had been sitting in the dark, and Dupin now arose for the purpose of lighting a lamp, but sat down again, without doing so, upon G——'s saying that he had called to
10 consult us, or rather to ask the opinion of my friend, about some official business which had occasioned a great deal of trouble.

"If it is any point requiring reflection," observed Dupin, as he forbore to enkindle the wick, "we shall
15 examine it to better purpose in the dark."

"That is another of your odd notions," said the Prefect, who had the fashion of calling everything "odd" that was beyond his comprehension, and thus lived amid an absolute legion of "oddities."

20 "Very true," said Dupin, as he supplied his visitor with a pipe and rolled toward him a comfortable chair.

"And what is the difficulty now?" I asked. "Nothing more in the assassination way, I hope?"

25 "Oh, no; nothing of that nature. The fact is, the business is very simple indeed, and I make no doubt that we can manage it sufficiently well ourselves; but then I thought Dupin would like to hear the details of it, because it is so excessively odd."

30 "Simple and odd?" said Dupin.

"Why, yes; and not that exactly either. The fact is, we have all been a good deal puzzled because the affair is so simple, and yet baffles us altogether."

"Perhaps it is the very simplicity of the thing which
35 puts you at fault," said my friend.

"What nonsense you do talk!" replied the Prefect, laughing heartily.

"Perhaps the mystery is a little too plain," said Dupin.

5   "Oh, good heavens! who ever heard of such an idea?"

"A little too self-evident."

"Ha! ha! ha!—ha! ha! ha!—ho! ho! ho!" roared our visitor, profoundly amused. "Oh, Dupin, you will be the death of me yet!"

10   "And what, after all, is the matter on hand?" I asked.

"Why I will tell you," replied the Prefect, as he gave a long, steady, and contemplative puff and settled himself in his chair—"I will tell you in a few words; but, before I begin, let me caution you that this is an affair 15 demanding the greatest secrecy, and that I should most probably lose the position I now hold were it known that I confided it to any one."

"Proceed," said I.

"Or not," said Dupin.

20   "Well, then; I have received personal information, from a very high quarter, that a certain document of the last importance has been purloined from the royal apartments. The individual who purloined it is known—this beyond a doubt; he was seen to take it. It is known, 25 also, that it still remains in his possession."

"How is this known?" asked Dupin.

"It is clearly inferred," replied the Prefect, "from the nature of the document and from the non-appearance of certain results which would at once arise from its 30 passing out of the robber's possession, that is to say, from his employing it as he must design in the end to employ it."

"Be a little more explicit," I said.

"Well, I may venture so far as to say that the paper 35 gives its holder a certain power in a certain quarter

where such power is immensely valuable." The Prefect
was fond of the cant of diplomacy.

"Still I do not quite understand," said Dupin.

"No? Well; the disclosure of the document to a third
5 person, who shall be nameless, would bring in question
the honor of a personage of most exalted station; and this
fact gives the holder of the document an ascendency over
the illustrious personage whose honor and peace are so
jeopardized."

10   "But this ascendency," I interposed, "would depend
upon the robber's knowledge of the loser's knowledge of
the robber. Who would dare——"

"The thief," said G——, "is the minister D——, who
dares all things, those unbecoming as well as those be-
15 coming a man. The method of the theft was not less
ingenious than bold. The document in question,—a letter, to be frank,—had been received by the personage
robbed while alone in the royal boudoir. During its
perusal she was suddenly interrupted by the entrance of
20 the other exalted personage from whom especially it was
her wish to conceal it. After a hurried and vain en-
deavor to thrust it in a drawer, she was forced to place it,
open as it was, upon a table. The address, however, was
uppermost, and, the contents thus unexposed, the letter
25 escaped notice. At this juncture enters the minister
D——. His lynx eye immediately perceives the paper,
recognizes the handwriting of the address, observes the
confusion of the personage addressed, and fathoms her
secret. After some business transactions hurried through
30 in his ordinary manner, he produces a letter somewhat
similar to the one in question, opens it, pretends to read
it, then places it in close juxtaposition to the other.
Again he converses for some fifteen minutes upon the
public affairs. At length, in taking leave, he takes also
35 from the table the letter to which he had no claim. Its

rightful owner saw, but, of course, dared not call attention to the act, in the presence of the third personage, who stood at her elbow. The minister decamped, leaving his own letter, one of no importance, upon the table."

5   "Here, then," said Dupin to me, "you have precisely what you demand to make the ascendency complete, the robber's knowledge of the loser's knowledge of the robber."

"Yes," replied the Prefect; "and the power thus attained has, for some months past, been wielded, for political purposes, to a very dangerous extent. The personage robbed is more thoroughly convinced every day of the necessity of reclaiming her letter. But this, of course, cannot be done openly. In fine, driven to despair, she has committed the matter to me."

"Than whom," said Dupin, amid a perfect whirlwind of smoke, "no more sagacious agent could, I suppose, be desired or even imagined."

"You flatter me," replied the Prefect; "but it is possible that some such opinion may have been entertained."

"It is clear," said I, "as you observe, that the letter is still in the possession of the minister; since it is this possession, and not any employment of the letter, which bestows the power. With the employment the power departs."

"True," said G——; "and upon this conviction I proceeded. My first care was to make thorough search of the minister's hotel; and here my chief embarrassment lay in the necessity of searching without his knowledge. Beyond all things, I have been warned of the danger which would result from giving him reason to suspect our design."

"But," said I, "you are quite *au fait* in these investigations. The Parisian police have done this thing often before."

"Oh, yes; and for this reason I did not despair. The
habits of the minister gave me, too, a great advantage.
He is frequently absent from home all night. His ser-
vants are by no means numerous. They sleep at a dis-
5 tance from their master's apartment, and, being chiefly
Neapolitans, are readily made drunk. I have keys, as
you know, with which I can open any chamber or cabinet
in Paris. For three months a night has not passed, during the greater part of which I have not been engaged,
10 personally, in ransacking the D—— Hotel. My honor
is interested, and, to mention a great secret, the reward is
enormous. So I did not abandon the search until I had
become fully satisfied that the thief is a more astute man
than myself. I fancy that I have investigated every
15 nook and corner of the premises in which it is possible
that the paper can be concealed."

"But is it not possible," I suggested, "that although
the letter may be in possession of the minister, as it un-
questionably is, he may have concealed it elsewhere than
20 upon his own premises?"

"This is barely possible," said Dupin. "The present
peculiar condition of affairs at court, and especially of
those intrigues in which D—— is known to be involved,
would render the instant availability of the document,
25 its susceptibility of being produced at a moment's notice,
a point of nearly equal importance with its possession."

"Its susceptibility of being produced?" said I.

"That is to say, of being destroyed," said Dupin.

"True," I observed. "The paper is clearly, then,
30 upon the premises. As for its being upon the person of
the minister, we may consider that as out of the question."

"Entirely," said the Prefect. "He has been twice
waylaid, as if by footpads, and his person rigidly searched
under my own inspection."

35   "You might have spared yourself this trouble," said

Dupin. "D——, I presume, is not altogether a fool, and,
if not, must have anticipated these waylayings, as a matter of course."

"Not altogether a fool," said G——, "but then he is
5 a poet, which I take to be only one remove from a fool."

"True," said Dupin, after a long and thoughtful whiff
from his meerschaum, "although I have been guilty of
certain doggerel myself."

"Suppose you detail," said I, "the particulars of your
10 search."

"Why, the fact is, we took our time, and we searched
everywhere. I have had long experience in these affairs.
I took the entire building, room by room; devoting the
nights of a whole week to each. We examined, first, the
15 furniture of each apartment. We opened every possible
drawer; and I presume you know that, to a properly
trained police-agent, such a thing as a 'secret' drawer is
impossible. Any man is a dolt who permits a 'secret'
drawer to escape him in a search of this kind. The
20 thing is so plain. There is a certain amount of bulk, of
space, to be accounted for in every cabinet. Then we
have accurate rules. The fiftieth part of a line could not
escape us. After the cabinets we took the chairs. The
cushions we probed with the fine long needles you have
25 seen me employ. From the tables we removed the tops."

"Why so?"

"Sometimes the top of a table or other similarly
arranged piece of furniture is removed by the person
wishing to conceal an article; then the leg is excavated,
30 the article deposited within the cavity, and the top replaced. The bottoms and tops of bedposts are employed
in the same way."

"But could not the cavity be detected by sounding?"
I asked.
35 "By no means if, when the article is deposited, a

sufficient wadding of cotton be placed around it. Besides, in our case, we were obliged to proceed without noise."

"But you could not have removed, you could not have taken to pieces all articles of furniture in which it
5 would have been possible to make a deposit in the manner you mention. A letter may be compressed into a thin spiral roll, not differing much in shape or bulk from a large knitting needle, and in this form it might be inserted into the rung of a chair, for example. You did
10 not take to pieces all the chairs?"

"Certainly not, but we did better: we examined the rungs of every chair in the hotel, and, indeed, the jointings of every description of furniture, by the aid of a most powerful microscope. Had there been any traces of
15 recent disturbance we should not have failed to detect it instantly. A single grain of gimlet-dust, for example, would have been as obvious as an apple. Any disorder in the gluing, any unusual gaping in the joints, would have sufficed to insure detection."

20   "I presume you looked to the mirrors, between the boards and the plates, and you probed the bed and the bedclothes, as well as the curtains and carpets."

"That of course; and when we had absolutely completed every particle of the furniture in this way, then we
25 examined the house itself. We divided its entire surface into compartments, which we numbered, so that none might be missed. Then we scrutinized each individual square inch throughout the premises, including the two houses immediately adjoining, with the microscope, as
30 before."

"The two houses adjoining!" I exclaimed; "you must have had a great deal of trouble."

"We had; but the reward offered is prodigious."

"You include the grounds about the houses?"

35   "All the grounds are paved with brick. They gave us

comparatively little trouble. We examined the moss between the bricks and found it undisturbed."

"You looked among D——'s papers, of course, and into the books of the library?"

5   "Certainly; we opened every package and parcel; we not only opened every book, but we turned over every leaf in each volume, not contenting ourselves with a mere shake, according to the fashion of some of our police officers. We also measured the thickness of every book-

10 cover with the most accurate admeasurement, and applied to each the most jealous scrutiny of the microscope. Had any of the bindings been recently meddled with, it would have been utterly impossible that the fact should have escaped observation. Some five or six volumes, just from

15 the hands of the binder, we carefully probed, longitudinally, with the needles."

"You explored the floors beneath the carpets?"

"Beyond doubt. We removed every carpet and examined the boards with a microscope."

20   "And the paper on the walls?"

"Yes."

"You looked into the cellars?"

"We did."

"Then," I said, "you have been making a miscalcula-

25 tion, and the letter is not upon the premises, as you suppose."

"I fear you are right there," said the Prefect. "And now, Dupin, what would you advise me to do?"

"To make a thorough research of the premises."

30   "That is absolutely needless," replied G——. "I am not more sure that I breathe than I am that the letter is not at the hotel."

"I have no better advice to give you," said Dupin. "You have, of course, an accurate description of the

35 letter?"

"Oh, yes!" and here the Prefect, producing a memo-randum-book, proceeded to read aloud a minute account of the internal, and especially of the external, appearance of the missing document. Soon after finishing the peru-
5 sal of this description he took his departure, more entirely depressed in spirits than I had ever known the good gentleman before.

In about a month afterward he paid us another visit, and found us occupied very nearly as before. He took
10 a pipe and a chair and entered into some ordinary con-versation. At length I said:

"Well, but, G——, what of the purloined letter? I presume you have at last made up your mind that there is no such thing as overreaching the Minister?"

15 "Confound him! say I—yes; I made the re-examina-tion, however, as Dupin suggested, but it was all labor lost, as I knew it would be."

"How much was the reward offered, did you say," asked Dupin.

20 "Why, a very great deal, a very liberal reward; I don't like to say how much, precisely; but one thing I will say,—that I wouldn't mind giving my individual check for fifty thousand francs to any one who could obtain me that letter. The fact is, it is becoming of more and
25 more importance every day; and the reward has been lately doubled. If it were trebled, however, I could do no more than I have done."

"Why, yes," said Dupin, drawlingly, between the whiffs of his meerschaum, "I really—think, G——,
30 you have not exerted yourself—to the utmost in this matter. You might—do a little more, I think, eh?"

"How? In what way?"

"Why — puff, puff — you might — puff, puff — em-ploy counsel in the matter, eh?—puff, puff, puff. Do you
35 remember the story of Abernethy?"

"No; hang Abernethy!"

"To be sure! hang him and welcome. But, once upon a time, a certain rich miser conceived the design of sponging upon this Abernethy for a medical opinion.
5 Getting up, for this purpose, an ordinary conversation in a private company, he insinuated his case to the physician as that of an imaginary individual.

"'We will suppose,' said the miser, 'that his symptoms are such and such; now, Doctor, what would you have
10 directed him to take?'

"'Take!' said Abernethy, 'why, take advice, to be sure!'"

"But," said the Prefect, a little discomposed, "I am perfectly willing to take advice and to pay for it. I
15 would really give fifty thousand francs to any one who would aid me in the matter."

"In that case," replied Dupin, opening a drawer and producing a check-book, "you may as well fill me up a check for the amount mentioned. When you have
20 signed it I will hand you the letter."

I was astounded. The Prefect appeared absolutely thunderstricken. For some minutes he remained speech-less and motionless, looking incredulously at my friend with open mouth, and eyes that seemed starting from
25 their sockets; then, apparently recovering himself in some measure, he seized a pen, and after several pauses and vacant stares finally filled up and signed a check for fifty thousand francs and handed it across the table to Dupin. The latter examined it carefully and deposited it in his
30 pocket book; then, unlocking an escritoire, took thence a letter and gave it to the Prefect. This functionary grasped it in a perfect agony of joy, opened it with a trembling hand, cast a rapid glance at its contents, and then, scrambling and struggling to the door, rushed at
35 length unceremoniously from the room and from the

house without having uttered a syllable since Dupin had
requested him to fill up the check.

When he had gone, my friend entered into some ex-
planations.

5   "The Parisian police," he said, "are exceedingly able
in their way. They are persevering, ingenious, cunning,
and thoroughly versed in the knowledge which their
duties seem chiefly to demand. Thus, when G—— de-
tailed to us his mode of searching the premises at the
10 Hotel D——, I felt entire confidence in his having made
a satisfactory investigation, so far as his labors extended."

"'So far as his labors extended'?" said I.

"Yes," said Dupin. "The measures adopted were not
only the best of their kind, but carried out to absolute
15 perfection. Had the letter been deposited within the
range of their search, these fellows would, beyond a question, have found it."

I merely laughed, but he seemed quite serious in all
that he said.

20   "The measures then," he continued, "were good in
their kind and well executed; their defect lay in their being
inapplicable to the case and to the man. A certain set
of highly ingenious resources are, with the Prefect, a
sort of Procrustean bed, to which he forcibly adapts his
25 designs. But he perpetually errs by being too deep or too
shallow for the matter in hand; and many a schoolboy is
a better reasoner than he. I knew one about eight years
of age, whose success at guessing in the game of 'even and
odd' attracted universal admiration. This game is sim-
30 ple, and is played with marbles. One player holds in his
hand a number of these toys and demands of another
whether that number is even or odd. If the guess is
right, the guesser wins one; if wrong, he loses one. The
boy to whom I allude won all the marbles of the school.
35 Of course he had some principle of guessing; and this lay

in mere observation and admeasurement of the astuteness
of his opponents. For example, an errant simpleton is
his opponent, and, holding up his closed hand, asks, 'Are
they even or odd?' Our schoolboy replies, 'Odd,' and
5 loses; but upon the second trial he wins, for he then says
to himself: 'The simpleton had them even upon the first
trial, and his amount of cunning is just sufficient to make
him have them odd upon the second; I will therefore
guess odd;' he guesses odd and wins. Now, with a sim-
10 pleton a degree above the first, he would have reasoned
thus: 'This fellow finds that in the first instance I guessed
odd, and in the second he will propose to himself, upon
the first impulse, a simple variation from even to odd, as
did the first simpleton; but then a second thought will
15 suggest that this is too simple a variation, and finally he
will decide upon putting it even as before. I will therefore guess even;'—he guesses even and wins. Now this
mode of reasoning in the schoolboy, whom his fellows
termed 'lucky'—what, in its last analysis, is it?"
20   "It is merely," I said, "an identification of the reasoner's intellect with that of his opponent."
    "It is," said Dupin; "and upon inquiring of the boy
by what means he effected the thorough identification in
which his success consisted, I received answer as follows:
25 'When I wish to find out how wise, or how stupid, or how
good, or how wicked is any one, or what are his thoughts
at the moment, I fashion the expression of my face, as
accurately as possible, in accordance with the expression
of his and then wait to see what thoughts or sentiments
30 arise in my mind or heart, as if to match or correspond
with the expression.' This response of the schoolboy lies
at the bottom of all the spurious profundity which has
been attributed to Rochefoucauld, to La Bruyère, to
Machiavelli, and to Campanella."
35   "And the identification," I said, "of the reasoner's

intellect with that of his opponent depends, if I understand you aright, upon the accuracy with which the opponent's intellect is admeasured."

"For its practical value it depends upon this," replied
5 Dupin; "and the Prefect and his cohort fail so frequently, first, by default of this identification, and, secondly, by ill-admeasurement, or rather through non-admeasurement, of the intellect with which they are engaged. They consider only their own ideas of ingenuity; and, in searching
10 for anything hidden, advert only to the modes in which they would have hidden it. They are right in this much, that their own ingenuity is a faithful representative of that of the mass; but when the cunning of the individual felon is diverse in character from their own the felon
15 foils them, of course. This always happens when it is above their own, and very usually when it is below. They have no variation of principle in their investigations; at best, when urged by some unusual emergency, by some extraordinary reward, they extend or exaggerate their old
20 modes of practice without touching their principles. What, for example, in this case of D——, has been done to vary the principle of action? What is all this boring, and probing, and sounding, and scrutinizing with the microscope, and dividing the surface of the building into
25 square inches; what is it all but an exaggeration of the application of the one principle or set of principles of search, which are based upon the one set of notions regarding human ingenuity, to which the Prefect, in the long routine of his duty, has been accustomed? Do you
30 not see he has taken it for granted that all men proceed to conceal a letter, not exactly in a gimlet-hole bored in a chair-leg, but, at least in some out-of-the-way hole or corner suggested by the same tenor of thought which would urge a man to secrete a letter in a gimlet-hole bored
35 in a chair-leg? And do you not see, also, that such *re-*

cherchés nooks for concealment are adapted only for ordinary occasions, and would be adopted only by ordinary intellects; for, in all cases of concealment, a disposal of the article concealed, a disposal of it in this *recherché*
5 manner, is, in the very first instance, presumable and presumed; and thus its discovery depends, not at all upon the acumen, but altogether upon the mere care, patience and determination of the seekers; and where the case is of importance, or, what amounts to the same thing in the
10 policial eyes, when the reward is of magnitude, the qualities in question have never been known to fail. You will now understand what I meant in suggesting that, had the purloined letter been hidden anywhere within the limits of the Prefect's examination,—in other words, had
15 the principle of its concealment been comprehended within the principles of the Prefect,—its discovery would have been a matter altogether beyond question. This functionary, however, has been thoroughly mystified; and the remote source of his defeat lies in the supposition that
20 the minister is a fool, because he has acquired renown as a poet. All fools are poets; this the Prefect feels; and he is merely guilty of a *non distributio medii* in thence inferring that all poets are fools."

"But is this really the poet?" I asked. "There are
25 two brothers, I know; and both have attained reputation in letters. The minister, I believe, has written learnedly on the Differential Calculus. He is a mathematician and no poet."

"You are mistaken; I know him well; he is both.
30 As poet and mathematician, he would reason well; as mere mathematician, he could not have reasoned at all, and thus would have been at the mercy of the Prefect."

"You surprise me," I said, "by these opinions, which have been contradicted by the voice of the world. You
35 do not mean to set at naught the well-digested idea of

centuries? The mathematical reason has long been regarded as the reason *par excellence.*"

"The mathematicians, I grant you, have done their
best to promulgate the popular error to which you allude,
5 and which is none the less an error for its promulgation as
truth."

"I mean to say," continued Dupin, while I merely
laughed at his last observations, "that if the minister had
been no more than a mathematician, the Prefect would
10 have been under no necessity of giving me this check. I
knew him, however, as both mathematician and poet, and
my measures were adapted to his capacity with reference
to the circumstances by which he was surrounded. I
knew him as a courtier, too, and as a bold *intriguant.*
15 Such a man, I considered, could not fail to be aware of the
ordinary policial modes of action. He could not have
failed to anticipate—and events have proved that he did
not fail to anticipate—the waylayings to which he was
subjected. He must have foreseen, I reflected, the secret
20 investigations of his premises. His frequent absences
from home at night, which were hailed by the Prefect as
certain aids to his success, I regarded only as ruses to
afford opportunity for thorough search to the police, and
thus the sooner to impress them with the conviction, to
25 which G——, in fact, did finally arrive,—the conviction
that the letter was not upon the premises. I felt, also,
that the whole train of thought, which I was at some
pains in detailing to you just now, concerning the invari-
able principle of policial action in searches for articles
30 concealed,—I felt that this whole train of thought would
necessarily pass through the mind of the minister. It
would imperatively lead him to despise all the ordinary
nooks of concealment. He could not, I reflected, be so
weak as not to see that the most intricate and remote
35 recess of his hotel would be as open as his commonest

closets to the eyes, to the probes, to the gimlets, and to
the microscopes of the Prefect. I saw, in fine, that he
would be driven, as a matter of course, to simplicity, if
not deliberately induced to it as a matter of choice. You
5 will remember, perhaps, how desperately the Prefect
laughed when I suggested, upon our first interview, that
it was just possible this mystery troubled him so much on
account of its being so very self-evident."

"Yes," said I, "I remember his merriment well. I
10 really thought he would have fallen into convulsions."

"The material world," continued Dupin, "abounds
with very strict analogies to the immaterial; and thus
some color of truth has been given to the rhetorical
dogma that metaphor, or simile, may be made to
15 strengthen an argument as well as to embellish a description. The principle of the *vis inertiæ*, for example,
seems to be identical in physics and metaphysics. It is
not more true in the former, that a large body is with
more difficulty set in motion than a smaller one, and that
20 its subsequent momentum is commensurate with this
difficulty, than it is, in the latter, that intellects of the
vaster capacity, while more forcible, more constant, and
more eventful in their movements than those of inferior
grade, are yet the less readily moved, and more em-
25 barrassed, and full of hesitation in the first few steps of
their progress. Again: have you ever noticed which of
the street signs, over the shop doors, are the most attrac-
tive of attention?"

"I have never given the matter a thought," I said.

30 "There is a game of puzzles," he resumed, "which is
played upon a map. One party playing requires another
to find a given word, the name of town, river, state or
empire—any word, in short, upon the motley and per-
plexed surface of the chart. A novice in the game gen-
35 erally seeks to embarrass his opponents by giving them

the most minutely lettered names; but the adept selects
such words as stretch, in large characters, from one end
of the chart to the other. These, like the over-largely
lettered signs and placards of the street, escape observa-
5 tion by dint of being excessively obvious; and here the
physical oversight is precisely analogous with the moral
inapprehension by which the intellect suffers to pass un-
noticed those considerations which are too obtrusively
and too palpably self-evident. But this is a point, it ap-
10 pears, somewhat above or beneath the understanding of the
Prefect. He never once thought it probable, or possible,
that the minister had deposited the letter immediately
beneath the nose of the whole world by way of best pre-
venting any portion of that world from perceiving it.

15   "But the more I reflected upon the daring, dashing,
and discriminating ingenuity of D——; upon the fact
that the document must always have been at hand, if he
intended to use it to good purpose; and upon the decisive
evidence, obtained by the Prefect, that it was not hidden
20 within the limits of that dignitary's ordinary search, the
more satisfied I became that, to conceal this letter, the
minister had resorted to the comprehensive and sagacious
expedient of not attempting to conceal it at all.

"Full of these ideas, I prepared myself with a pair of
25 green spectacles, and called one fine morning, quite by
accident, at the ministerial hotel. I found D—— at
home, yawning, lounging, and dawdling, as usual, and
pretending to be in the last extremity of *ennui*. He is,
perhaps, the most really energetic human being now
30 alive; but that is only when nobody sees him.

"To be even with him, I complained of my weak eyes,
and lamented the necessity of the spectacles, under cover
of which I cautiously and thoroughly surveyed the whole
apartment, while seemingly intent only upon the conver-
35 sation of my host.

"I paid especial attention to a large writing-table near
which he sat, and upon which lay confusedly some mis-
cellaneous letters and other papers, with one or two musical instruments and a few books. Here, however, after
5 a long and very deliberate scrutiny, I saw nothing to
excite particular suspicion.

"At length my eyes, in going the circuit of the room,
fell upon a trumpery filigree card-rack of pasteboard, that
hung dangling by a dirty blue ribbon from a little brass
10 knob just beneath the middle of the mantelpiece. In
this rack, which had three or four compartments, were
five or six visiting-cards and a solitary letter. This last
was much soiled and crumpled. It was torn nearly in
two, across the middle, as if a design, in the first instance,
15 to tear it entirely up as worthless, had been altered, or
stayed, in the second. It had a large black seal, bearing
the D—— cipher very conspicuously, and was addressed,
in a diminutive female hand, to D——, the minister,
himself. It was thrust carelessly, and even, as it seemed,
20 contemptuously, into one of the uppermost divisions of
the rack.

"No sooner had I glanced at this letter than I con-
cluded it to be that of which I was in search. To be
sure, it was, to all appearance, radically different from the
25 one of which the Prefect had read us so minute a description. Here the seal was large and black, with the D——
cipher; there it was small and red, with the ducal arms
of the S—— family. Here, the address, to the minister,
was diminutive and feminine; there the superscription, to
30 a certain royal personage, was markedly bold and decided; the size alone formed a point of correspondence.
But, then, the radicalness of these differences, which was
excessive: the dirt; the soiled and torn condition of the
paper, so inconsistent with the true methodical habits
35 of D——, and so suggestive of a design to delude the be-

holder into an idea of the worthlessness of the document,—these things, together with the hyperobtrusive
situation of this document, full in the view of every
visitor, and thus exactly in accordance with the conclu-
5 sions to which I had previously arrived; these things, I
say, were strongly corroborative of suspicion, in one who
came with the intention to suspect.

"I protracted my visit as long as possible, and, while
I maintained a most animated discussion with the min-
10 ister upon a topic which I knew well had never failed to
interest and excite him, I kept my attention really riveted
upon the letter. In this examination, I committed to
memory its external appearance and arrangement in the
rack; and also fell, at length, upon a discovery which set
15 at rest whatever trivial doubt I might have entertained.
In scrutinizing the edges of the paper, I observed them to
be more chafed than seemed necessary. They presented
the broken appearance which is manifested when a stiff
paper, having been once folded and pressed with a folder,
20 is refolded in a reversed direction, in the same creases or
edges which had formed the original fold. This discovery
was sufficient. It was clear to me that the letter had
been turned, as a glove, inside out, redirected and re-
sealed. I bade the minister good-morning, and took my
25 departure at once, leaving a gold snuff-box upon the table.

"The next morning I called for the snuff-box, when we
resumed, quite eagerly, the conversation of the preceding
day. While thus engaged, however, a loud report, as if of
a pistol, was heard immediately beneath the windows of
30 the hotel, and was succeeded by a series of fearful screams
and the shoutings of a terrified mob. D—— rushed to a
casement, threw it open, and looked out. In the meantime I stepped to the card-rack, took the letter, put it in
my pocket, and replaced it by a facsimile (so far as re-
35 gards externals) which I had carefully prepared at my

lodgings, imitating the D—— cipher very readily by means of a seal formed of bread.

"The disturbance in the street had been occasioned by the frantic behavior of a man with a musket. He had 5 fired it among a crowd of women and children. It proved, however, to have been without a ball, and the fellow was suffered to go his way as a lunatic or a drunkard. When he had gone, D—— came from the window, whither I had followed him immediately upon securing 10 the object in view. Soon afterward I bade him farewell. The pretended lunatic was a man in my own pay."

"But what purpose had you," I asked, "in replacing the letter by a facsimile? Would it not have been better, at the first visit, to have seized it openly and de-15 parted?"

"D——," replied Dupin, "is a desperate man, and a man of nerve. His hotel, too, is not without attendants devoted to his interests. Had I made the wild attempt you suggest I might never have left the ministerial pres-20 ence alive. The good people of Paris might have heard of me no more. But I had an object apart from these considerations. You know my political prepossessions. In this matter I act as a partisan of the lady concerned. For eighteen months the minister has had her in his 25 power. She has now him in hers, since, being unaware that the letter is not in his possession, he will proceed with his exactions as if it was. Thus will he inevitably commit himself at once to his political destruction. His downfall, too, will not be more precipitate than awkward. 30 In the present instance I have no sympathy, at least no pity, for him who descends. He is that *monstrum horrendum*, an unprincipled man of genius. I confess, however, that I should like very well to know the precise character of his thoughts, when, being defied by her 35 whom the Prefect terms 'a certain personage,' he is reduced to opening the letter which I left for him in the card-rack."

"How? Did you put anything particular in it?"

"Why, it did not seem altogether right to leave the
5 interior blank—that would have been insulting. D——, at Vienna once, did me an evil turn, which I told him, quite good-humoredly, I should remember. So, as I knew he would feel some curiosity in regard to the identity of the person who had outwitted him, I thought it a pity
10 not to give him a clew. He is well acquainted with my MS., and I just copied into the middle of the blank sheet the words:—

'——Un dessein si funestre,
S'il n'est digne d'Atrée, est digne de Thyeste.'

15 They are to be found in Crébillon's 'Atrée.'"

NOTES AND SUGGESTIONS

A narrative may be related by the writer in three different ways: first, he may tell the story in the first person as though the events had happened to himself; second, he may tell it from the point of view of an onlooker (this is a difficult method to handle, for the author must account for the narrator's ability to know of all of the happenings); third, he may tell it in the third person, assuming that the writer is in a position to know all things. The last is the method most frequently adopted.

1. Which of these methods has Poe used in this story?

2. Which has been used in "The Legend of Sleepy Hollow"?

3. a. What is the name of the character who tells this story?
   b. Why is the fact that we really know nothing about this man, immaterial?

4. a. Where does the action of this story begin?
   b. Compare the opening of this tale with the opening of "The Legend of Sleepy Hollow."
   c. Which of the two will be more apt to secure an immediate interest?
   d. Give reasons for your answer.

5. Compare the description of the characters in this story, with the description of those in "The Legend." Note in this selection: first, the lack of humor; second, the lack of figurative constructions.

6. See if you can explain why it is that the action of this story is rapid.

7. a. Where does the climax of the story come?

   b. Point out the specific paragraph.

   c. Why is it not a fault, in this case, that the climax does not come near the end of the story?

8. Summarize Poe's method of telling a story and contrast it with Irving's.

Explanatory Notes

Page 48, line 35—"Abernethy"—John Abernethy, a celebrated English surgeon, was born in London in 1764. He was famous as a lecturer and made many improvements in surgery. He was noted also for his shrewdness and wit.

Page 50, line 24—"Procrustean"—pertaining to Procrustes, a Greek highwayman who fitted his victims to an iron bed by stretching out or cutting off their legs as the case required.

Page 51, lines 33 and 34—"Rochefoucauld"—a French writer and teacher. He was born in Paris in 1613 and is known in literature through his maxims, his memoirs and his correspondence.

"La Bruyère"—a French moralist. He was born in Paris in 1645. He studied law and later held several diplomatic positions. He was appointed tutor to the young Duke of Bourbon.

"Machiavelli"—a famous Italian statesman. He was born in Florence in 1469. His skill in foreign affairs caused him to be employed as minister at foreign courts. He was the author of several works on the subject of statesmanship.

"Campanella"—a Dominican monk. He was born in Italy in 1568. He was a philosopher and a pioneer of modern thought.

Page 53, line 22—"non distributio medii"—undistributed middle—a fallacy in logic.

Page 54, line 2—"par excellence"—a partly naturalized phrase from the French, meaning through or by way of great merit or superiority.

Page 55, line 16—"vis inertiæ"—a Latin term meaning the force of inertia. Inertia, in physics, is the resistance of matter to a change of state.

Page 56, line 28—"ennui"—a mental weariness produced by lack of interest.

Page 60, lines 13 and 14—These lines occur in Crébillon's "Atrée et Thyeste," fourth scene of the fifth act. Look up the story of the two brothers in any classical dictionary.

Suggestions for Home Reading

Poe's "Gold Bug"—a tale of mystery in which the deciphering of a cryptogram plays an important part.

Poe's "Murders in Rue Morgue" —introducing the great detective, Dupin.

Stevenson's "The New Arabian Nights"—tales of mystery, told in Stevenson's masterly fashion.

DAVID SWAN

BY NATHANIEL HAWTHORNE

NATHANIEL HAWTHORNE was born in Massachusetts in 1804 and died in New Hampshire in 1864. He is generally conceded to be the greatest American novelist. He was a graduate of Bowdoin College. At various times during his life he held governmental positions but devoted most of his time to literary work. Probably the most widely read of his books is "The Scarlet Letter."

The story given here is one of Hawthorne's "Twice Told Tales." It is a splendid example of this writer's unity of structure and his purity of style. Notice in reading it, how smoothly the paragraphs have been formed and what a wonderful command of language the author has.

WE can be but partially acquainted even with the events which actually influence our course through life and our final destiny. There are innumerable other events, if such they may be called, which come close upon
5 us, yet pass away without actual results or even betraying their near approach by the reflection of any light or shadow across our minds. Could we know all the vicissitudes of our fortunes, life would be too full of hope and fear, exultation or disappointment, to afford us a single
10 hour of true serenity. This idea may be illustrated by a page from the secret history of David Swan.

We have nothing to do with David until we find him, at the age of twenty, on the high road from his native place to the city of Boston, where his uncle, a small dealer in the grocery line, was to take him behind the counter.

5 Be it enough to say that he was a native of New Hampshire, born of respectable parents, and had received an ordinary school education with a classic finish by a year at Gilmanton Academy. After journeying on foot from sunrise till nearly noon of a summer's day, his weariness

10 and the increasing heat determined him to sit down in the first convenient shade and await the coming up of the stage-coach. As if planted on purpose for him, there soon appeared a little tuft of maples with a delightful recess in the midst, and such a fresh, bubbling spring that

15 it seemed never to have sparkled for any wayfarer but David Swan. Virgin or not, he kissed it with his thirsty lips and then flung himself along the brink, pillowing his head upon some shirts and a pair of pantaloons tied up in a striped cotton handkerchief. The sunbeams could

20 not reach him; the dust did not yet rise from the road after the heavy rain of yesterday, and his grassy lair suited the young man better than a bed of down. The spring murmured drowsily beside him; the branches waved dreamily across the blue sky overhead, and a

25 deep sleep, perchance hiding dreams within its depths, fell upon David Swan. But we are to relate events which he did not dream of.

While he lay sound asleep in the shade other people were wide awake, and passed to and fro, afoot, on horse-

30 back and in all sorts of vehicles, along the sunny road by his bedchamber. Some looked neither to the right hand nor the left and knew not that he was there; some merely glanced that way without admitting the slumberer among their busy thoughts; some laughed to see how soundly he

35 slept, and several whose hearts were brimming full of

scorn ejected their venomous superfluity on David Swan. A middle-aged widow, when nobody else was near, thrust her head a little way into the recess, and vowed that the young fellow looked charming in his sleep. A temperance
5 lecturer saw him, and wrought poor David into the texture of his evening's discourse as an awful instance of dead drunkenness by the roadside.

But censure, praise, merriment, scorn and indifference were all one—or, rather, all nothing—to David Swan. He
10 had slept only a few moments when a brown carriage drawn by a handsome pair of horses bowled easily along and was brought to a standstill nearly in front of David's resting-place. A linch-pin had fallen out and permitted one of the wheels to slide off. The damage was slight
15 and occasioned merely a momentary alarm to an elderly merchant and his wife, who were returning to Boston in the carriage. While the coachman and a servant were replacing the wheel the lady and gentleman sheltered themselves beneath the maple trees, and there espied the
20 bubbling fountain and David Swan asleep beside it. Impressed with the awe which the humblest sleeper usually sheds around him, the merchant trod as lightly as the gout would allow, and his spouse took good heed not to rustle her silk gown lest David should start up all
25 of a sudden.

"How soundly he sleeps!" whispered the old gentleman. "From what a depth he draws that easy breath! Such sleep as that, brought on without an opiate, would be worth more to me than half my income, for it would
30 suppose health and an untroubled mind."

"And youth besides," said the lady. "Healthy and quiet age does not sleep thus. Our slumber is no more like his than our wakefulness."

The longer they looked, the more did this elderly
35 couple feel interested in the unknown youth to whom the

wayside and the maple shade were as a secret chamber
with the rich gloom of damask curtains brooding over
him. Perceiving that a stray sunbeam glimmered down
upon his face, the lady contrived to twist a branch aside
5 so as to intercept it, and, having done this little act of
kindness, she began to feel like a mother to him.

"Providence seems to have laid him here," whispered
she to her husband, "and to have brought us hither to
find him, after our disappointment in our cousin's son.
10 Methinks I can see a likeness to our departed Henry.
Shall we waken him?"

"To what purpose?" said the merchant, hesitating.
"We know nothing of the youth's character."

"That open countenance!" replied his wife, in the
15 same hushed voice, yet earnestly. "This innocent sleep!"

While these whispers were passing, the sleeper's heart
did not throb, nor his breath become agitated, nor his
features betray the least token of interest. Yet Fortune
was bending over him just ready to let fall a burden of
20 gold. The old merchant had lost his only son, and had
no heir to his wealth except a distant relative with whose
conduct he was dissatisfied. In such cases people sometimes do stranger things than to act the magician and
awaken a young man to splendor who fell asleep in
25 poverty.

"Shall we not waken him?" repeated the lady, per-
suasively.

"The coach is ready, sir," said the servant, behind.

The old couple started, reddened and hurried away,
30 mutually wondering that they should ever have dreamed
of doing anything so very ridiculous. The merchant
threw himself back in the carriage and occupied his mind
with the plan of a magnificent asylum for unfortunate
men of business. Meanwhile, David Swan enjoyed his
35 nap.

The carriage could not have gone above a mile or two
when a pretty young girl came along with a tripping pace
which showed precisely how her little heart was dancing
in her bosom. Perhaps it was this merry kind of motion
5 that caused her garter to slip its knot. Conscious that
the silken girth—if silk it were—was relaxing its hold, she
turned aside into the shelter of the maple trees, and there
found a young man asleep by the spring. Blushing as
red as any rose that she should have intruded into a gen-
10 tleman's bedchamber, and for such a purpose too, she
was about to make her escape on tiptoe. But there was
peril near the sleeper. A monster of a bee had been
wandering overhead—buzz, buzz, buzz—now among the
leaves, now flashing through the strips of sunshine, and
15 now lost in the dark shade, till finally he appeared to be
settling on the eyelid of David Swan. The sting of a bee
is sometimes deadly. As free-hearted as she was innocent, the girl attacked the intruder with her handkerchief,
brushed him soundly and drove him from beneath the
20 maple shade. How sweet a picture! This good deed accomplished, with quickened breath and a deeper blush
she stole a glance at the youthful stranger for whom she
had been battling with a dragon in the air.

"He is handsome!" thought she, and blushed redder
25 yet.

How could it be that no dream of bliss grew so strong
within him that, shattered by its very strength, it should
part asunder and allow him to perceive the girl among its
phantoms? Why, at least, did no smile of welcome
30 brighten upon his face? She was come, the maid whose
soul, according to the old and beautiful idea, had been
severed from his own, and whom in all his vague but passionate desires he yearned to meet. Her only could he
love with a perfect love, him only could she receive into
35 the depths of her heart, and now her image was faintly

blushing in the fountain by his side; should it pass away, its happy luster would never gleam upon his life again.

"How sound he sleeps!" murmured the girl. She departed, but did not trip along the road so lightly as when
5 she came.

Now, this girl's father was a thriving country merchant in the neighborhood, and happened at that identical time to be looking out for just such a young man as David Swan. Had David formed a wayside acquaint-
10 ance with the daughter, he would have become the father's clerk, and all else in natural succession. So here, again, had good fortune, the best of fortunes, stolen so near that her garments brushed against him, and he knew nothing of the matter.

15 The girl was hardly out of sight when two men turned aside beneath the maple shade. Both had dark faces set off by cloth caps, which were drawn down aslant over their brows. Their dresses were shabby, yet had a certain smartness. These were a couple of rascals who got
20 their living by whatever the devil sent them, and now, in the interim of other business, had staked the joint profits of their next piece of villainy on a game of cards which was to have been decided here under the trees. But, finding David asleep by the spring, one of the rogues whis-
25 pered to his fellow:

"Hist! Do you see that bundle under his head?"

The other villain nodded, winked and leered.

"I'll bet you a horn of brandy," said the first, "that the chap has either a pocketbook or a snug little hoard of
30 small change stowed away amongst his shirts. And if not there, we will find it in his pantaloons pocket."

"But how if he wakes?" said the other.

His companion thrust aside his waistcoat, pointed to the handle of a dirk and nodded.

35 "So be it!" muttered the second villain.

They approached the unconscious David, and, while
one pointed the dagger toward his heart, the other began
to search the bundle beneath his head. Their two faces,
grim, wrinkled and ghastly with guilt and fear, bent over
5 their victim, looking horrible enough to be mistaken for
fiends should he suddenly awake. Nay, had the villains
glanced aside into the spring, even they would hardly
have known themselves as reflected there. But David
Swan had never worn a more tranquil aspect, even when
10 asleep on his mother's breast.

"I must take away the bundle," whispered one.

"If he stirs, I'll strike," muttered the other.

But at this moment a dog scenting along the ground
came in beneath the maple trees and gazed alternately at
15 each of these wicked men and then at the quiet sleeper.
He then lapped out of the fountain.

"Pshaw!" said one villain.   "We can do nothing now.
The dog's master must be close behind."

"Let's take a drink and be off," said the other.

20   The man with the dagger thrust back the weapon into
his bosom and drew forth a pocket pistol, but not of that
kind which kills by a single discharge. It was a flask of
liquor with a block-tin tumbler screwed upon the mouth.
Each drank a comfortable dram, and left the spot with so
25 many jests and such laughter at their unaccomplished
wickedness that they might be said to have gone on their
way rejoicing. In a few hours they had forgotten the
whole affair, nor once imagined that the recording angel
had written down the crime of murder against their souls
30 in letters as durable as eternity. As for David Swan, he
still slept quietly, neither conscious of the shadow of
death when it hung over him nor of the glow of renewed
life when that shadow was withdrawn. He slept, but no
longer so quietly as at first. An hour's repose had
35 snatched from his elastic frame the weariness with which

many hours of toil had burdened it. Now he stirred,
now moved his lips without a sound, now talked in an
inward tone to the noonday specters of his dream. But
a noise of wheels came rattling louder and louder along
5 the road, until it dashed through the dispersing mist of
David's slumber; and there was the stage-coach. He
started up with all his ideas about him.

"Halloo, driver! Take a passenger?" shouted he.

"Room on top!" answered the driver.

10 Up mounted David, and bowled away merrily toward
Boston without so much as a parting glance at that fountain of dreamlike vicissitude. He knew not that a phan-
tom of Wealth had thrown a golden hue upon its waters,
nor that one of Love had sighed softly to their murmur,
15 nor that one of Death had threatened to crimson them with
his blood, all in the brief hour since he lay down to sleep.
Sleeping or waking, we hear not the airy footsteps of
the strange things that almost happen. Does it not argue
a superintending Providence that, while viewless and un-
20 expected events thrust themselves continually athwart
our path, there should still be regularity enough in mortal
life to render foresight even partially available?

NOTES AND SUGGESTIONS

1. What is the purpose of the first paragraph?

2. Where does this story begin?

3. Trace the action of the story.

4. a. What would have been the result, in each case, had David been aroused by the old couple?
   b. By the girl?
   c. By the robbers?

5. a. What, in each case, settled the question?
   Note that these deciding factors were of no importance in themselves.
   b. Tell why the author makes use of them.

6. Point out the climax of the story.

7. a. Why did David stop?
   b. What finally caused him to awaken?

8. Note carefully how the writer keeps to his story. What do we call this quality of style?

9. Compare the sentences of this selection with those of "The Purloined Letter," as to their length.

10. Read the sentences of the second paragraph, one by one.

a. What have you to say about their length?

b. Mention all the things that are told you in the first sentence, then in the second and so on through the entire paragraph. It is very unusual to be told so much in single sentences.

c. How does the author do it so clearly?

11. a. Compare Hawthorne's description of the merchant with Irving's description of Ichabod.

b. How does Hawthorne bring out the traits of character in the various persons figuring in the tale?

12. a. Compare the last paragraph with the first.

b. Show the purpose of the last paragraph.

13. Comment upon the author's use of words in the last paragraph.

A DISSERTATION ON ROAST PIG

BY CHARLES LAMB

CHARLES LAMB was born in London in 1775 and died in Edmonton in 1834. He was a noted man of letters, critic and humorist. He had a very ordinary schooling, after which he became a clerk in a large commercial house. His whole life, apart from his work, was devoted to the care of his sister, who was subject to fits of insanity. He was the intimate friend of the most famous authors of his day; his unselfishness, his modesty and his gentle wit endeared him to all who knew him. His kindly, lovable nature shows through all of his writings.

"A Dissertation on Roast Pig" is one of a collection of essays signed "Elia" and written at various times for the London Magazine. When these sketches were published in book form they were called "Essays of Elia." They are characterized by quaint humor.

MANKIND, says a Chinese manuscript, which my
friend M—— was obliging enough to read and explain to
me, for the first seventy thousand ages ate their meat raw,
clawing or biting it from the living animal, just as they do
5 in Abyssinia to this day. This period is not obscurely
hinted at by their great Confucius in the second chapter
of his "Mundane Mutations," where he designates a kind
of golden age by the term Cho-fang, literally the Cooks'
Holiday. The manuscript goes on to say that the art of
10 roasting, or rather broiling (which I take to be the elder
brother) was accidentally discovered in the manner
following: The swineherd, Ho-ti, having gone out into the
woods one morning, as his manner was, to collect mast
for his hogs, left his cottage in the care of his eldest son,
15 Bo-bo, a great, lubberly boy, who, being fond of playing
with fire as younkers of his age commonly are, let some
sparks escape into a bundle of straw, which, kindling
quickly, spread the conflagration over every part of their
poor mansion, till it was reduced to ashes. Together with
20 the cottage (a sorry, antediluvian makeshift of a building,
you may think it), what was of much more importance,
a fine litter of new-farrowed pigs, no less than nine in
number, perished. China pigs have been esteemed a
luxury all over the East, from the remotest periods that
25 we read of. Bo-bo was in utmost consternation, as you
may think, not so much for the sake of the tenement,
which his father and he could easily build up again with
a few dry branches, and the labor of an hour or two, at
any time, as for the loss of the pigs. While he was think-
30 ing what he should say to his father, and wringing his
hands over the smoking remnants of one of those untimely sufferers, an odor assailed his nostrils, unlike any
scent which he had before experienced. What could it
proceed from?—not from the burned cottage—he had
35 smelt-that smell before—indeed, this was by no means

the first accident of the kind which had occurred through
the negligence of this unlucky young fire-brand. Much
less did it resemble that of any known herb, weed, or
flower. A premonitory moistening at the same time
5 overflowed his nether lip. He knew not what to think.
He next stooped down to feel the pig, if there were any
signs of life in it. He burned his fingers, and to cool them
he applied them in his booby fashion to his mouth. Some
of the crumbs of the scorched skin had come away with
10 his fingers, and for the first time in his life (in the world's
life, indeed, for before him no man had known it) he
tasted—*crackling!* Again he felt and fumbled at the pig.
It did not burn him so much now, still he licked his
fingers from a sort of habit. The truth at length broke
15 into his slow understanding that it was the pig that
smelt so, and the pig that tasted so delicious; and sur-
rendering himself up to the new-born pleasure, he fell to
tearing up whole handfuls of the scorched skin with the
flesh next it, and was cramming it down his throat in his
20 beastly fashion, when his sire entered amid the smoking
rafters, armed with retributory cudgel, and finding how
affairs stood, began to rain blows upon the young rogue's
shoulders, as thick as hailstones, which Bo-bo heeded not
any more than if they had been flies. The tickling pleas-
25 ure which he experienced in his lower regions had rendered him quite callous to any inconveniences he might feel
in those remote quarters. His father might lay on, but
he could not beat him from his pig, till he had fairly made
an end of it, when, becoming a little more sensible of his
30 situation, something like the following dialogue ensued:
    "You graceless whelp, what have you got there de-
vouring? Is it not enough that you have burned me
down three houses with your dog's tricks, and be hanged
to you! but you must be eating fire, and I know not what
35 —what have you got there, I say?"

"O father, the pig, the pig! do come and taste how nice the burnt pig eats!"

The ears of Ho-ti tingled with horror. He cursed his son, and he cursed himself, that ever he should beget a
5 son that should eat burnt pig.

Bo-bo, whose scent was wonderfully sharpened since morning, soon raked out another pig, and fairly rending it asunder, thrust the lesser half by main force into the fists of Ho-ti, still shouting out, "Eat, eat, eat the burnt
10 pig, father, only taste—O Lord!"—with such-like barbarous ejaculations, cramming all the while as if he would choke.

Ho-ti trembled every joint while he grasped the abominable thing, wavering whether he should not put
15 his son to death for an unnatural young monster, when the crackling scorching his fingers, as it had done his son's, and applying the same remedy to them, he in his turn tasted some of its flavor, which, make what sour mouths he would for pretense, proved not altogether displeasing
20 to him. In conclusion (for the manuscript here is a little tedious) both father and son fairly set down to the mess, and never left off till they had dispatched all that remained of the litter.

Bo-bo was strictly enjoined not to let the secret
25 escape, for the neighbors would certainly have stoned them for a couple of abominable wretches, who could think of improving upon the good meat which God had sent them. Nevertheless, strange stories got about. It was observed that Ho-ti's cottage was burnt down now
30 more frequently than ever. Nothing but fires from this time forward. Some would break out in broad day, others in the night time. As often as the sow farrowed, so sure was the house of Ho-ti to be in a blaze; and Ho-ti himself, which was the more remarkable, instead of chas-
35 tising his son, seemed to grow more indulgent to him than

ever. At length they were watched, the terrible mystery
discovered, and father and son summoned to take their
trial at Pekin, then an inconsiderable assize town. Evidence was given, the obnoxious food itself produced in
5 court, and verdict about to be pronounced, when the
foreman of the jury begged that some of the burnt pig,
of which the culprits stood accused, might be handed
into the box. He handled it, and they all handled it;
and burning their fingers, as Bo-bo and his father had
10 done before them, and Nature prompting to each of them
the same remedy, against the face of all the facts, and the
clearest charge which judge had ever given—to the surprise of the whole court, townsfolk, strangers, reporters,
and all present—without leaving the box, or any manner
15 of consultation whatever, they brought in a simultaneous
verdict of Not Guilty.

The judge, who was a shrewd fellow, winked at the
manifest iniquity of the decision; and when the court was
dismissed, went privily and bought up all the pigs that
20 could be had for love or money. In a few days his Lord-
ship's town-house was observed to be on fire. The thing
took wing, and now there was nothing to be seen but fire
in every direction. Fuel and pigs grew enormously dear
all over the district. The insurance offices, one and all,
25 shut up shop. People built slighter and slighter every
day, until it was feared that the very science of architecture would, in no long time, be lost to the world. Thus
this custom of firing houses continued, till in process of
time, says my manuscript, a sage arose, like our Locke,
30 who made a discovery, that the flesh of swine, or indeed,
of any other animal, might be cooked (burnt, as they
called it) without the necessity of consuming a whole
house to dress it. Then first began the rude form of gridiron. Roasting by the string or spit came in a century
35 or two later, I forget in whose dynasty. By such slow

degrees, concludes the manuscript, do the most useful, and seemingly the most obvious arts, make their way among mankind: —

5 Without placing too implicit faith in the account above given, it must be agreed that, if a worthy pretext for so dangerous an experiment as setting houses on fire (especially in these days) could be assigned in favor of any culinary object, that pretext and excuse, might be found in *roast pig*.

10 Of all the delicacies in the whole *mundus edibilis*, I will maintain it to be the most delicate—*princeps obsoniorum*.

I speak not of your grown porkers—things between pig and pork—those hobbydehoys, but a young and ten-
15 der suckling, under a moon old, guiltless, as yet, of the sty, with no original speck of the *amor immunditiæ*, the hereditary failing of the first parent, yet manifest, his voice, as yet, not broken, but something between a childish treble and a grumble, the mild forerunner, or
20 *præludium* of a grunt.

He must be roasted. I am not ignorant that our ancestors ate them seethed, or boiled—but what a sacrifice of the exterior tegument!

There is no flavor comparable, I will contend, to that
25 of the crisp, tawny, well-watched, not over-roasted crackling, as it is well called—the very teeth are invited to their share of the pleasure at this banquet in overcoming the coy, brittle resistance—with the adhesive oleaginous—oh, call it not fat! but an indefinable sweetness
30 growing up to it—the tender blossoming of fat—fat cropped in the bud—taken in the shoot—in the first innocence—the cream and quintessence of the child-pig's yet pure food—the lean, no lean, but a kind of animal manna—or rather fat and lean (if it must
35 be so), so blended and running into each other, that

both together make but one ambrosian result or common substance.

Behold him, while he is "doing"—it seemeth rather a
refreshing warmth, than a scorching heat, that he is so
5 passive to. How equably he twirleth round the string!
Now he is just done. To see the extreme sensibility of
that tender age! he hath wept out his pretty eyes—
radiant jellies—shooting-stars.

See him in the dish, his second cradle, how meek he
10 lieth!—wouldst thou have had this innocent grow up to
the grossness and indocility which too often accompany
maturer swinehood? Ten to one he would have proved
a glutton, a sloven, an obstinate, disagreeable animal
—wallowing in all manner of filthy conversation—from
15 these sins he is happily snatched away—

> "Ere sin could blight or sorrow fade;
>   Death came with timely care——"

His memory is odoriferous; no clown curseth while his
stomach half rejecteth the rank bacon, no coal-heaver
20 bolteth him in reeking sausages; he hath a fair sepulcher
in the grateful stomach of the judicious epicure, and for
such a tomb might be content to die.

I am one of those who freely and ungrudgingly impart
a share of the good things of this life which fall to their
25 lot (few as mine are in this kind) to a friend. I protest
I take as great an interest in my friend's pleasures, his
relishes, and proper satisfactions, as in mine own. "Presents," I often say, "endear Absents." Hares, pheasants,
partridges, snipes, barn-door chickens (those "tame vil-
30 latic fowl"), capons, plovers, brawn, barrels of oysters, I
dispense as freely as I receive them. I love to taste them,
as it were, upon the tongue of my friend. But a stop
must be put somewhere. One would not, like Lear,
"give everything." I make my stand upon pig. Me-

thinks it is an ingratitude to the Giver of all good
flavors, to extra-domiciliate, or send out of the house,
slightingly (under pretext of friendship, or I know not
what), a blessing so particularly adapted, predestined,
5 I may say, to my individual palate. It argues an insen-
sibility.

I remember a touch of conscience in this kind at
school. My good old aunt, who never parted from me
at the end of a holiday without stuffing a sweetmeat, or
10 some nice thing into my pocket, had dismissed me one
evening with a smoking plum-cake, fresh from the oven.
In my way to school (it was over London bridge), a gray-
headed old beggar saluted me (I have no doubt, at this
time of day, that he was a counterfeit). I had no pence
15 to console him with, and in the vanity of self-denial, and
the very coxcombry of charity, schoolboy-like, I made him
a present of—the whole cake! I walked on a little,
buoyed up, as one is on such occasions, with a sweet
soothing of self-satisfaction; but before I had got to the
20 end of the bridge my better feelings returned, and I
burst into tears, thinking how ungrateful I had been to
my good aunt, to go and give her good gift away to a
stranger that I had never seen before, and who might be
a bad man for aught I knew; and then I thought of the
25 pleasure my aunt would be taking in thinking that I—I
myself and not another—would eat her nice cake, and
what should I say to her the next time I saw her, how
naughty I was to part with her pretty present!—and the
odor of that spicy cake came back upon my recollection,
30 and the pleasure and the curiosity I had taken in seeing
her make it, and her joy when she had sent it to the oven,
and how disappointed she would feel that I had never
had a bit of it in my mouth at last—and I blamed my
impertinent spirit of almsgiving, and out-of-place hypoc-
35 risy of goodness; and above all, I wished never to see the

face again of that insidious, good-for-nothing, old gray impostor.

Our ancestors were nice in their method of sacrificing these tender victims. We read of pigs whipped to death,
5 with something of a shock, as we hear of any other obsolete custom. The age of discipline is gone by, or it would be curious to inquire (in a philosophical light merely) what effect this process might have toward intenerating and dulcifying a substance naturally so mild and dulcet
10 as the flesh of young pigs. It looks like refining a violet. Yet we should be cautious, while we condemn the inhumanity, how we censure the wisdom of the practice. It might impart a gusto.

I remember an hypothesis, argued upon by the young
15 students when I was at St. Omer's, and maintained with much learning and pleasantry on both sides, "Whether, supposing that the flavor of a pig who obtained his death by whipping (*per flaggellationem extremam*) superadded a pleasure upon the palate of a man more intense than
20 any possible suffering we can conceive in the animal, is man justified in using that method of putting the animal to death?" I forget the decision.

His sauce should be considered. Decidedly, a few bread-crumbs, done up with his liver and brains, and a
25 dash of mild sage. But banish, dear Mrs. Cook, I beseech you, the whole onion tribe. Barbecue your whole hogs to your palate, steep them in shalots, stuff them out with plantations of the rank and guilty garlic; you cannot poison them, or make them stronger than they are—but
30 consider, he is a weakling—a flower.

NOTES AND SUGGESTIONS

An Essay is a form of composition in which a writer sets forth his views on a certain subject. It is not so formal nor so exhaustive as a treatise. This kind of composition is termed exposition.

1. What is the purpose of this essay?
2. What is the writer's taste in regard to "roast pig"?
3. How does the author attempt to trace the origin of roasting pigs?
4. a. Tell briefly what was in the Chinese manuscript?
   b. In what spirit does the author offer this historical account of the "art" of roasting?
5. Note the quaint humor in the following expressions: "China pigs have been esteemed a luxury all over the East from the remotest periods we read of"; "—— wringing his hands over the smoking remains of those untimely sufferers"; "a premonitory moistening overflowed his nether lip." Point out other instances of the same kind.
6. Note that when the author has finished his historical account of the development of this art, he begins to set forth his own views. In the paragraphs beginning on line 10, page 75, and line 13, same page, Lamb makes use of a number of Latin terms.
   a. Why does he do this?
   b. What is the effect gained thereby?
7. In the paragraph beginning on line 24, page 75, pick out the metaphors used. (Note throughout the selection how frequently Lamb makes use of this figure of speech.)
8. What does the next paragraph (beginning line 3, page 76) describe?
9. a. Note the effect of the one that follows. (Beginning line 9, page 76.)
   b. How does the author gain this effect?
10. a. Repeat in your own words the writer's reminiscence about his aunt and the plum-cake.
    b. Why does Lamb put in that incident? (If you can not tell at once, read the two preceding paragraphs, and then see if you can find the reason.)
11. In olden times how did cooks make pigs more tender?
12. What do you think of the sentence—"It looks like refining a violet," in its application to the topic under consideration?
13. What was the subject for debate, mentioned in the paragraph beginning line 14, page 78?
14. From your study of this selection, make a brief summary of the qualities of Lamb's style of writing.

Explanatory Notes

Page 71, line 6—"Confucius"—a celebrated Chinese philosopher. He was born about 551 B. C. in Lu (modern province of Shantung). His teachings, written in books partly by himself and partly by his followers, are looked upon by the Chinese much as the Bible is by Christian nations.

Page 71, line 20—"antediluvian" —of or pertaining to times or things or events, before the great flood in the days of Noah.

Page 74, line 3—"assize town"— a town in which regular sessions of a superior court are held.

Page 74, line 29—"Locke"—a celebrated English philosopher. He was born in 1632 and died in 1704. He was one of the most influential thinkers of modern times. His chief work is his "Essay on the Human Understanding."

Page 75, line 10—"mundus edibilis"—a Latin phrase meaning "the world of eatables" i.e., every thing that is good to eat.

Page 75, line 11—"princeps obsoniorum"—a L a t i n expression meaning, "the chief of delicacies."

Page 75, line 16—"amor immunditiæ"—a Latin expression, meaning "a love of filth."

Page 75, line 20—"præludium"— a Latin word; præ, meaning "before" and, ludus, "play." In music, this word refers to a strain, introducing the chief theme.

Page 78, line 18—"per flaggellationem extremam"—a Latin phrase, meaning, "by whipping to death."

Suggestions for Home Reading

Mark Twain's "Tom Sawyer"— a boys' story, humorously told. Dickens' "Pickwick Papers"— sketches setting forth incidents in the lives of Pickwick and his friends.

SAN FRANCISCO

(A Modern Cosmopolis)

BY ROBERT LOUIS STEVENSON

ROBERT LOUIS STEVENSON was born in Scotland in 1850 and died in Samoa in 1894. He came of a family of culture and refinement. He had the advantage of a splendid education. Because of ill health, a great part of his life was spent in travel in Europe, America, Australia and among the South Sea Islands.

Sidney Colvin summarizes the literary work of Stevenson in the following words: "Without being the inventor of any new form or mode of literary art, he handled with success and freshness nearly all the old forms—the moral, critical and personal essay, travels, sentimental and other, romances and short tales, both historical and modern, tales of mystery, boys' stories of adventure, drama, and lyrical and meditative verse. To some of these forms he gave quite new life; through all alike he expressed vividly his own extremely personal way of seeing and being, his peculiar sense of nature and romance.

"No man ever gained truer friends through the practice of an art; and to these, the art in all its perfectness, was but as a country, rich, varied, where they might walk and know him—the story running an accompaniment, like a singing brook by the path, or pounding like a tempestuous sea on the shoulders of the cliff, where they lay, sheltered and by the fire.

"He made a broad appeal; seven men in one, and of a radiant heart, his sympathy, his breadth of judgment, and his love of men, gave him that noble comprehension of life that makes the Christmas sermon a new gospel.

"Brave friend! young men and unspoiled women are thy lovers, and the earth is sweet with thy memory."

San Francisco (A Modern Cosmopolis) was written by Stevenson after a sojourn of some months there in the years 1879 and 1880. In reading this essay it is well to keep in mind the following facts: A Spanish town was laid out on the present site of San Francisco in the year 1835. A United States man-of-war took possession of it in 1846. It became a place of importance because of the discovery of gold in California in 1848 and grew with wonderful rapidity. In 1850 it was incorporated as a city. Devastating fires occurred in 1849 and 1851, and a frightful earthquake and fire caused great loss of life and property in 1906.

THE Pacific coast of the United States, as you may see by the map, and still better in that admirable book, "Two Years Before the Mast," by Dana, is one of the most exposed and shelterless on earth. The trade-
5 wind blows fresh; the huge Pacific swell booms along

degree after degree of an unbroken line of coast. South
of the joint firth of the Columbia and Willamette, there
flows in no considerable river; south of Puget Sound there
is no protected inlet of the ocean. Along the whole sea-
5 board of California there are but two unexceptionable
anchorages, the bight of the bay of Monterey, and the
inland sea that takes its name from San Francisco.

Whether or not it was here that Drake put in in 1597,
we cannot tell. There is no other place so suitable; and
10 yet the narrative of Francis Pretty scarcely seems to suit
the features of the scene. Viewed from seaward, the
Golden Gates should give no very English impression to
justify the name of a New Albion. On the west, the deep
lies open; nothing near but the still vexed Farrallones.
15 The coast is rough and barren. Tamalpais, a mountain
of memorable figure, springing direct from the sea-level,
over-plumbs the narrow entrance from the north. On the
south, the loud music of the Pacific sounds along beaches
and cliffs, and among broken reefs, the sporting place of
20 the sea-lion. Dismal, shifting sand hills, wrinkled by the
wind, appear behind. Perhaps, too, in the days of Drake,
Tamalpais would be clothed to its peak with the majestic
redwoods.

Within the memory of persons not yet old, a mariner
25 might have steered into these narrows—not yet the
Golden Gates—opened out the surface of the bay—here
girt with hills, there lying broad to the horizon—and beheld a scene as empty of the presence, as pure from the
handiworks of man, as in the days of our old sea-com-
30 mander. A Spanish mission, fort, and church took the
place of those "houses of the people of the country"
which were seen by Pretty, "close to the waterside."
All else would be unchanged. Now, a generation later, a
great city covers the sand-hills on the west, a growing
35 town lies along the muddy shallows of the east; steam-

boats pant continually between them from before sunrise
till the small hours of the morning; lines of great sea-
going ships lie ranged at anchor; colors fly upon the
islands; and from all around the hum of corporate life, of
5 beaten bells, and steam, and running carriages, goes
cheerily abroad in the sunshine. Choose a place on one
of the huge, throbbing ferry-boats, and, when you are
midway between the city and the suburb, look around.
The air is fresh and salt as if you were at sea. On the
10 one hand is Oakland, gleaming white among its gardens.
On the other, to seaward, hill after hill is crowded and
crowned with the palaces of San Francisco; its long streets
lie in regular bars of darkness, east and west, across the
sparkling picture; a forest of masts bristles like bul-
15 rushes about its feet; nothing remains of the days of
Drake but the faithful tradewind scattering the smoke,
the fogs that will begin to muster about sundown, and
the fine bulk of Tamalpais looking down on San Francisco, like Arthur's Seat on Edinburgh.
20   Thus in the course of a generation only, this city and
its suburb have arisen. Men are alive by the score who
have hunted all over the foundations in a dreary waste.
I have dined near the "punctual center" of San Francisco with a gentleman (then newly married) who told
25 me of his former pleasures, wading with his fowling-piece
in sand and scrub, on the site of the house where we were
dining. In this busy, moving generation, we have all
known cities to cover our boyish playgrounds, we have
all started for a country walk and stumbled on a new
30 suburb; but I wonder what enchantment of the "Arabian
Nights" can have equalled this evocation of a roaring
city, in a few years of a man's life from the marshes and
the blowing sand. Such swiftness of increase, as with an
overgrown youth, suggests a corresponding swiftness of
35 destruction. The sandy peninsular of San Francisco,

mirroring itself on one side in the bay, beaten, on the
other, by the surge of the Pacific, and shaken to the heart
by frequent earthquakes, seems in itself no very durable
foundation. According to Indian tales, perhaps older
5 than the name of California, it once rose out of the sea in
a moment, and some time or other shall, in a moment,
sink again. No Indian, they say, cares to linger on that
dreadful land. "The earth hath bubbles as the water has,
and this is of them." Here, indeed, all is new, nature as
10 well as towns. The very hills of California have an un-
finished look; the rains and the streams have not yet
carved them to their perfect shape. The forests spring
like mushrooms from the unexhausted soil; and they are
mown down yearly by forest fires. We are in early geo-
15 logical epochs, changeful and insecure; and we feel, as
with a sculptor's model, that the author may yet grow
weary of and shatter the rough sketch.

Fancy apart, San Francisco is a city beleaguered with
alarms. The lower parts, along the bay side, sit on piles:
20 old wrecks decaying, fish dwelling unsunned, beneath the
populous houses; and a trifling subsidence might drown
the business quarters in an hour. Earthquakes are not
uncommon, they are sometimes threatening in their violence; the fear of them grows yearly on a resident; he
25 begins with indifference, ends in sheer panic; and no one
feels safe in any but a wooden house. Hence it comes
that, in that rainless clime, the whole city is built of timber—a woodyard of unusual extent and complication;
that fires spring up readily, and, served by the unwearying
30 tradewind, swiftly spread; that all over the city there are
fire-signal boxes; that the sound of the bell, telling the
number of the threatened ward, is soon familiar to the
ear; and that nowhere else in the world is the art of the
fireman carried to so nice a point.
35   Next, perhaps, in order of strangeness to the speed of

its appearance, is the mingling of the races that combine
to people it. The town is essentially not Anglo-Saxon;
still more essentially not American. The Yankee and
the Englishman find themselves alike in a strange coun-
5 try. There are none of those touches—not of nature, and
I dare scarcely say of art—by which the Anglo-Saxon
feels himself at home in so great a diversity of lands.
Here, on the contrary, are airs of Marseilles and of Pekin.
The shops along the street are like the consulates of dif-
10 ferent nations. The passers-by vary in feature like the
slides of a magic-lantern. For we are here in that city
of gold to which adventurers congregated out of all the
winds of heaven; we are in a land that till the other day
was ruled and peopled by the countrymen of Cortez;
15 and the sea that laves the piers of San Francisco is the
ocean of the east and of the isles of summer. There goes
the Mexican, unmistakable; there the blue-clad China-
man with his white slippers; there the soft-spoken brown
Kanaka, or perhaps a waif from far-away Malaya. You
20 hear French, German, Italian, Spanish, and English in-
differently. You taste the food of all nations in the various restaurants; passing from a French *prixe-fixe*, where
every one is French, to a roaring German ordinary where
every one is German; ending, perhaps, in a cool and silent
25 Chinese tea-house. For every man, for every race and
nation, that city is a foreign city, humming with foreign
tongues and customs; and yet each and all have made
themselves at home. The Germans have a German
theater and innumerable beer-gardens. The French Fall
30 of the Bastile is celebrated with squibs and banners and
marching patriots, as noisily as the American Fourth of
July. The Italians have their dear domestic quarter,
with Italian caricatures in the windows, Chianti and
polenta in the taverns. The Chinese are as settled as in
35 China. The goods they offer for sale are as foreign as the

lettering on the signboard of the shop; dried fish from the
China seas; pale cakes and sweetmeats—the like, perhaps,
once eaten by Badroulbadour; nuts of unfriendly shape;
ambiguous, outlandish vegetables, misshapen, lean or bul-
5 bous—telling of a country where the trees are not as our
trees, and the very back garden is a cabinet of curiosities.
The joss-house is hard by, heavy with incense, packed
with quaint carvings and the paraphernalia of a foreign
ceremonial.   All these you behold, crowded together in
10 the narrower arteries of the city, cool, sunless, a little
mouldy, with the high, musical sing-song of that alien
language in your ears.   Yet the houses are of Occidental
build: the lines of a hundred telegraphs pass, thick as a
ship's rigging, overhead, a kite hanging among them per-
15 haps, or perhaps two; one European, one Chinese in shape
and color; mercantile Jack, the Italian fisher, the Dutch
merchant, the Mexican vaquero go hustling by; at the
sunny end of the street, a thoroughfare roars with European traffic; and meanwhile high and clear, out breaks,
20 perhaps, the San Francisco fire alarm, and people pause
to count the strokes, and in the stations of the double
fire-service you know that the electric bells are ringing,
the traps opening and clapping to, and the engine, manned
and harnessed, being whisked into the street, before the
25 sound of the alarm had ceased to vibrate on your ear.
Of all romantic places for a boy to loiter in, that Chinese
quarter is the most romantic.   There, on a half holiday,
three doors from home, he may visit an actual foreign
land, foreign in people, language, things and customs.
30 The very barber of the "Arabian Nights" shall be at
work before him, shaving heads; he shall see Aladdin
playing on the streets; who knows, but among those nameless vegetables, the fruit of the nose-tree itself may be
exposed for sale?   And the interest is heightened with a
35 chill of horror.   Below, you hear, the cellars are alive

with mystery; opium dens, where the smokers lie one
above another, shelf above shelf, close-packed and grovel-
ling in deadly stupor; the seats of unknown vices and
cruelties, the prisons of unacknowledged slaves and the
5 secret lazarettos of disease.

With all this mass of nationalities, crime is common.
Amid such a competition of respectabilities, the moral
sense is confused; in this camp of gold-seekers, speech is
loud and the hand is ready. There are rough quarters
10 where it is dangerous o' nights; cellars of public entertainment which the weary pleasure seeker chooses to
avoid. Concealed weapons are unlawful, but the law is
continually broken. One editor was shot dead while I
was there; another walked the streets accompanied by a
15 bravo, his guardian angel. I have been quietly eating a
dish of oysters in a restaurant where, not more than ten
minutes after I had left, shots were exchanged and took
effect; and one night about ten o'clock, I saw a man standing watchfully at a street-corner with a long Smith-and-
20 Wesson glittering in his hand behind his back. Somebody had done something he should not, and was being
looked for with a vengeance. It is odd, too, that the seat
of the last vigilance committee I know of—a mediæval
Vehmgericht—was none other than the Palace Hotel, the
25 world's greatest caravanserai, served by lifts and lighted
with electricity; where, in the great glazed court, a band
nightly discourses music from a grove of palms. So do
extremes meet in this city of contrasts: extremes of wealth
and poverty, apathy and excitement, the conveniences of
30 civilization and the red justice of Judge Lynch. The
streets lie straight up and down the hills and straight
across at right angles, these in the sun, those in the
shadow, a trenchant pattern of gloom and glare; and what
with the crisp illumination, the sea-air singing in your
35 ears, the chill and glitter, the changing aspects both of

things and people, the fresh sights at every corner of your
walk—sights of the bay, of Tamalpais, of steep, descending streets, of the outspread city—whiffs of alien speech,
sailors singing on shipboard, Chinese coolies toiling on the
5 shore, crowds brawling all day in the street before the
Stock Exchange—one brief impression follows another
and the city leaves upon the mind no general and stable
picture, but a profusion of airy and incongruous images,
of the sea and shore, the east and west, the summer and
10 the winter.

In the better parts of this most interesting city there
is apt to be a touch of the commonplace. It is in the
slums and suburbs that the city dilettante finds his game,
and there is nothing more characteristic and original than
15 the outlying quarters of San Francisco. The Chinese district is the most famous; but it is far from the only truffle
in the pie. There is another dingy corner, many a young
antiquity, many a *terrain vague* with that stamp of quaint-
ness that a city lover seeks and dwells on; and the indefi-
20 nite prolongation of its streets, up hill and down dale,
makes San Francisco a place apart. The same street in
its career visits and unites many different classes of society, here echoing with drays, there lying decorously
silent between the mansions of bonanza millionaires to
25 founder at last among the drifting sands beside Lone
Mountain cemetery, or die out among the sheds and lumber of the north. Thus you may be struck with a spot—
set it down for the most romantic in the city—and, glancing at the name-plate, find it is on the same street that you
30 yourself inhabit in another quarter of the town.

The great net of straight thoroughfares lying at right
angles east and west and north and south, over the shoulders of Nob Hill, the hill of palaces, must certainly be
counted the best part of San Francisco. It is there that
35 the millionaires are gathered together, vieing with each

other in display; looking down upon the business wards of
the city. That is California Street. Far away down you
may pick out a building with a little belfry; and that is
the Stock Exchange, the heart of San Francisco; a great
5 pump, we might call it, continually pumping up the sav-
ings of the lower quarters into the pockets of the millionaires upon the hill. But these same thoroughfares that
enjoy for a while so elegant a destiny have their lines prolonged into more unpleasant places. Some meet their fate
10 in the sands; some must take a cruise in the ill-famed
China quarters; some run into the sea; some perish un-
wept among pig-stys and rubbish heaps.

Nob Hill comes, of right, in the place of honor; but
the two other hills of San Francisco are more entertaining
15 to explore. On both there are a world of wooden houses
snoozing away all forgotten. Some are of the quaintest
design, others only romantic by neglect and age. Some
are curiously painted, and I have seen one at least with
ancient carvings panelled in its wall. Surely they are not
20 of Californian building, but far voyages from round the
stormy Horn, like those who sent for them and dwelt in
them at first. Brought to be the favorites of the wealthy,
they have sunk into these poor, forgotten districts, where,
like old town toasts, they keep each other silent counte-
25 nance. Telegraph Hill and Rincon Hill, these are the
dozing quarters that I recommend to the city dilettante.
There stand these forgotten houses, enjoying the unbroken sun and quiet. There, if there were such an
author, would the San Francisco Fortune du Boisgobey
30 pitch the first chapter of his mystery. But the first is
the quainter of the two. Visited under the broad natural daylight, and with the relief and accent of reality,
these scenes have a quality of dreamland and of the best
pages of Dickens. Telegraph Hill, besides, commands a
35 noble view; and as it stands at the turn of the bay, its

skirts are all waterside, and round from North Reach to
the Bay Front you can follow doubtful paths from one
quaint corner to another. Everywhere the same tumble-
down decay and sloppy progress, new things yet unmade,
5 old things tottering to their fall; everywhere the same out-
at-elbows, many-nationed loungers at dim, irregular grog-
shops; everywhere the same sea-air and isletted sea-pros-
pect; and for a last and more romantic note, you have on
the one hand Tamalpais standing high in the blue air, and
10 on the other the tail of that long alignment of three-
masted, full-rigged, deep-sea ships that make a forest of
spars along the eastern front of San Francisco. In no
other port is such a navy congregated. For the coast
trade is so trifling, and the ocean trade from round the
15 Horn so large, that the smaller ships are swallowed up,
and can do nothing to confuse the majestic order of these
merchant princes. In an age when the ship-of-the-line is
already a thing of the past, and we can never hope to go
coasting in a cock-boat between the "wooden walls" of a
20 squadron at anchor, there is perhaps no place on earth
where the power and beauty of sea architecture can be so
perfectly enjoyed as in this bay.

NOTES AND SUGGESTIONS

This essay is a piece of purely descriptive writing. It consists of
ten paragraphs.

1. Make an outline of the entire selection, giving the topic of each paragraph.

2. Note the orderly fashion in which Stevenson develops his subject. See if you can trace the connection between the paragraphs. This writer was a master of style. A study of his methods will help you to gain clearness in your composition work. It is splendid practice to try to imitate some of his paragraphs.

3. What ideas does Stevenson express concerning the first topic?

4. Third Paragraph; what are some of the changes

caused by the rapid growth of the city?

5. Fourth Paragraph; how does the writer emphasize the fact that this place grew rapidly?

6. a. To what unusual dangers is this city subject?

   b. In regard to each danger, tell why.

7. In regard to the population:

   a. What nationalities does the author speak of?

   b. Why does he speak of the varieties of cooking?

8. a. Repeat, in your own words, what Stevenson says about crime, in this place.

   b. How does he explain this condition?

   c. How does he emphasize the point he makes?

9. a. What sections of the city does he mention?

   b. Name the three hills he speaks of.

10. a. What does he say of the architecture?

    b. Of the shipping in the harbor?

Explanatory Notes

Page 83, line 19—"Arthur's Seat" —a hill over 800 feet high which overlooks Edinburgh from the East.

Page 84, line 8—"the earth hath bubbles"—a quotation from Shakespeare's "Macbeth," Act I, Sc. 3.

Page 85, line 19—"Kanaka"— the Kanakas were the aboriginal inhabitants of the Hawaiian Islands.

Page 85, line 29—"the Fall of the Bastile"—the Bastile was a prison fortress built in Paris in 1369 and destroyed on July 14, 1789, during an uprising of the people. July 14 has since been made a national holiday in France.

Page 85, line 33—"Chianti"—a red wine of Tuscany.

"polenta"—a porridge made from meal; it is the chief article of food for the poorer classes of Italians.

Page 86, line 3—"Badroulbadour" —the wife of Aladdin in the story of "Aladdin and the Wonderful Lamp," in "The Arabian Nights' Entertainment."

Page 87, line 24—"Vehmgericht" —mediæval tribunals which flourished in Germany in the 14th and 15th centuries. The sessions were open when civil matters were brought before them for adjudication; but secret, when criminal cases were tried.

Page 87, line 30—"Judge Lynch" —the origin of the term is doubtful. It is a way of speaking of the practice of condemning an accused person without forms of law.

Page 89, line 29—"du Boisgobey" —Fortune du Boisgobey was

born in 1821 and died in 1891. He was a French novelist who wrote a number of books on the criminal life in Paris.

Suggestions for Home Reading

Irving's "Westminster Abbey"— another example of this kind of writing.

White's "Gold"—an interesting and instructive account of the discovery of gold in California. It gives a very realistic picture of the conditions that existed in San Francisco during the first years of its existence.

THE TOURNAMENT AT ASHBY

(From "Ivanhoe")

BY SIR WALTER SCOTT

SIR WALTER SCOTT was a poet and novelist. He was born in Scotland in 1771 and died in Abbotsford in 1832. Lameness, the result of an early sickness, kept him from taking part in the usual pastimes of boyhood and caused him to spend much of his time in reading. In this way he stored his mind with a great deal of the material on which he drew in writing his ballads and romances. Through his writings, Scott gained distinction and wealth. In 1862, however, an unfortunate business connection caused him to lose all his money and burdened him with a debt which he felt bound in conscience to pay. His struggle to relieve himself of this burden caused a breakdown in mind and body from which he did not recover.

Scott was gifted with a wonderful power of story-telling and an unusual skill in the delineation of Character. There are many faults in his style but they are due in part, at least, to the rapidity with which he worked.

Of all of Sir Walter Scott's novels, "Ivanhoe" is probably the most widely read. The incidents of the story take place in England, during the reign of Richard I. In reading the novel it is well to keep in mind the following historical facts: Richard joined the Third Crusade; he left England with a host of English knights, journeyed to the Holy Land and there sought to regain Jerusalem from the infidels. Through treachery and jealousy, his allies, the

French and German nobles, withheld their aid and the expedition failed. When Richard was returning to England, he was taken prisoner by the Duke of Austria and delivered into the custody of his enemy, the Emperor of the Germans, Henry VI. For many months he was held in prison for ransom. The king's brother, Prince John, ruled in England during the absence of Richard. As he desired to retain possession of the crown he did nothing to set his brother free.

To understand the extract from "Ivanhoe" given here, it is necessary to know something of the whole story. The action of the piece is centered in four important scenes; the tournament at Ashby, the incidents in Sherwood Forest, the storming of the Norman castle and the trial of the Jewess. There are minor scenes which lead up to and connect the important ones. In the opening chapters of the novel we have been told the following story: An important Saxon lord, Cedric by name, disowned his son, the Knight of Ivanhoe, because he insisted upon following King Richard to the Holy Land, against his father's wishes. The ward of Cedric, the Lady Rowena, shows her interest in Ivanhoe by attempting to verify rumors which she has heard, telling of his return to England. The Norman nobles plot to aid Prince John in his efforts to gain the crown, and one of these, Sir Brian de Bois-Guilbert, shows an especial enmity towards Ivanhoe.

In order to increase his popularity, Prince John has ordered a three days' tournament to be held at Ashby for the entertainment of all classes. The gathering of the people, to attend this festival, serves the author with the means for introducing the characters important in the story. During the first day of the tournament, a knight who has refused to disclose his identity, has met and defeated in single combat all of the most renowned warriors amongst the Norman ranks.

MORNING arose in unclouded splendor, and ere the sun was much above the horizon, the idlest or the most eager of the spectators appeared on the common, moving to the lists as to a general center, in order to secure a fa-
5 vorable situation for viewing the continuation of the expected games.

The marshals and their attendants appeared next on
the field, together with the heralds, for the purpose of
receiving the names of the knights who intended to
joust, with the side which each chose to espouse. This
5 was a necessary precaution, in order to secure equality
betwixt the two bodies who should be opposed to each
other.

According to due formality, the Disinherited Knight
was to be considered as leader of the one body, while
10 Brian de Bois-Guilbert, who had been rated as having
done second best in the preceding day, was named first
champion of the other band. Those who had concurred
in the challenge adhered to his party, of course, excepting
only Ralph de Vipont, whom his fall had rendered unfit so
15 soon to put on his armor. There was no want of distinguished and noble candidates to fill up the ranks on
either side.

In fact, although the general tournament, in which all
knights fought at once, was more dangerous than single
20 encounters, they were, nevertheless, more frequented and
practised by the chivalry of the age. Many knights, who
had not sufficient confidence in their own skill to defy a
single adversary of high reputation, were, nevertheless,
desirous of displaying their valor in the general combat,
25 where they might meet others with whom they were more
upon an equality. On the present occasion, about fifty
knights were inscribed as desirous of combating upon
each side, when the marshals declared that no more could
be admitted, to the disappointment of several who were
30 too late in preferring their claim to be included.

About the hour of ten o'clock the whole plain was
crowded with horsemen, horsewomen and foot passengers
hastening to the tournament; and shortly after, a grand
flourish of trumpets announced Prince John and his
35 retinue, attended by many of those knights who meant to

take share in the game, as well as others who had no such
intention.

About the same time arrived Cedric the Saxon, with
the Lady Rowena, unattended, however, by Athelstane.
5 This Saxon lord had arrayed his tall and strong person in
armor in order to take his place among the combatants;
and, considerably to the surprise of Cedric, had chosen to
enlist himself on the part of the Knight Templar. The
Saxon, indeed, had remonstrated strongly with his friend
10 upon the injudicious choice he had made of his party; but
he had only received that sort of answer usually given by
those who are more obstinate in following their own
course, than strong in justifying it.

His best, if not his only reason, for adhering to the
15 party of Brian de Bois-Guilbert, Athelstane had the pru-
dence to keep to himself. Though his apathy of disposition prevented his taking any means to recommend himself to the Lady Rowena, he was, nevertheless, by no
means insensible to her charms, and considered his union
20 with her as a matter already fixed beyond doubt by the
assent of Cedric and her other friends. It had, therefore,
been with smothered displeasure that the proud, though
indolent, Lord of Coningsburgh beheld the victor of the
preceding day select Rowena as the object of that honor
25 which it became his privilege to confer. In order to pun-
ish him for a preference which seemed to interfere with his
own suit, Athelstane, confident of his strength, and to
whom his flatterers, at least, ascribed great skill in arms,
had determined not only to deprive the Disinherited
30 Knight of his powerful succor, but, if an opportunity
should occur, to make him feel the weight of his battle-axe.

De Bracy, and other knights attached to Prince John,
in obedience to a hint from him, had joined the party of
the challengers, John being desirous to secure, if possible,
35 the victory to that side. On the other hand, many other

knights, both English and Norman, natives and strangers,
took part against the challengers, the more readily that
the opposite band was to be led by so distinguished a
champion as the Disinherited Knight had approved
5 himself.

As soon as Prince John observed that the destined
Queen of the day had arrived upon the field, assuming
that air of courtesy which sat well upon him when he was
pleased to exhibit it, he rode forward to meet her, doffed
10 his bonnet, and, alighting from his horse, assisted the Lady
Rowena from her saddle, while his followers uncovered at
the same time, and one of the most distinguished dismounted to hold her palfrey.

"It is thus," said Prince John, "that we set the dutiful
15 example of loyalty to the Queen of Love and Beauty, and
are ourselves her guide to the throne which she must this
day occupy. Ladies," he said, "attend your Queen,
as you wish in your turn to be distinguished by like
honors."

20   So saying, the Prince marshalled Rowena to the seat
of honor opposite his own, while the fairest and most distinguished ladies present crowded after her to obtain
places as near as possible to their temporary sovereign.

No sooner was Rowena seated, than a burst of music,
25 half drowned by the shouts of the multitude, greeted her
new dignity. Meantime, the sun shone fierce and bright
upon the polished arms of the knights of either side, who
crowded the opposite extremities of the lists, and held
eager conference together concerning the best mode of
30 arranging their line of battle, and supporting the conflict.

The heralds then proclaimed silence until the laws of
the tourney should be rehearsed. These were calculated
in some degree to abate the dangers of the day; a precaution the more necessary, as the conflict was to be main-
35 tained with sharp swords and pointed lances.

The champions were therefore prohibited to thrust
with the sword, and were confined to striking. A knight,
it was announced, might use a mace or battle-axe at
pleasure, but the dagger was a prohibited weapon. A
5 knight unhorsed might renew the fight on foot with any
other on the opposite side in the same predicament; but
mounted horsemen were in that case forbidden to assail
him. When any knight could force his antagonist to the
extremity of the lists, so as to touch the palisade with his
10 person or arms, such opponent was obliged to yield himself vanquished, and his armor and horse were placed at
the disposal of the conqueror. A knight thus overcome
was not permitted to take farther share in the combat.
If any combatant was struck down, and unable to recover
15 his feet, his squire or page might enter the lists, and drag
his master out of the press; but in that case the knight was
adjudged vanquished, and his arms and horse declared
forfeited. The combat was to cease as soon as Prince
John should throw down his leading staff, or truncheon;
20 another precaution usually taken to prevent the unnecessary effusion of blood by the too long endurance of a
sport so desperate. Any knight breaking the rules of the
tournament, or otherwise transgressing the rules of honor-
able chivalry, was liable to be stripped of his arms, and,
25 having his shield reversed, to be placed in that posture
astride upon the bars of the palisade, and exposed to
public derision, in punishment of his unknightly conduct.
Having announced these precautions, the heralds con-
cluded with an exhortation to each knight to do his
30 duty, and to merit favor from the Queen of Beauty and
of Love.

This proclamation having been made, the heralds withdrew to their stations. The knights, entering at either
ends of the lists in long procession, arranged themselves
35 in a double file, precisely opposite to each other, the leader

of each party being in the center of the foremost rank, a
post which he did not occupy until each had carefully
arranged the ranks of his party, and stationed every one
in his place.

5   It was a goodly, and at the same time an anxious sight,
to behold so many gallant champions, mounted bravely,
and armed richly, stand ready prepared for an encounter
so formidable, seated on their war saddles like so many
pillars of iron, and awaiting the signal of encounter with
10 the same ardor as their generous steeds, which, by neigh-
ing and pawing the ground, gave signal of their im-
patience.

As yet the knights held their long lances upright, their
bright points glancing to the sun, and the streamers with
15 which they were decorated fluttering over the plumage
of the helmets. Thus they remained while the marshals
of the field surveyed their ranks with the utmost exact-
ness, lest either party had more or fewer than the
appointed number.   The tale was found exactly complete.
20 The marshals then withdrew from the lists, and William
de Wyvil, with a voice of thunder, pronounced the signal
words—*laissez aller!*   The trumpets sounded as he spoke
—the spears of the champions were at once lowered and
placed in the rests—the spurs were dashed into the flanks
25 of the horses, and the two foremost ranks of either party
rushed upon each other in full gallop, and met in the middle of the lists with a shock, the sound of which was heard
at a mile's distance.   The rear rank of each party ad-
vanced at a slower pace to sustain the defeated, and fol-
30 low up the success of the victors of their party.

The consequences of the encounter were not instantly
seen, for the dust raised by the trampling of so many
steeds darkened the air, and it was a minute ere the anxious spectators could see the fate of the encounter. When
35 the fight became visible, half the knights on each side were

dismounted, some by the dexterity of their adversary's
lance,—some by the superior weight and strength of opponents, which had borne down both horse and man,—
some lay stretched on earth as if never more to rise,—some
5 had already gained their feet, and were closing hand to
hand with those of their antagonists who were in the same
predicament,—and several on both sides, who had received
wounds by which they were disabled, were stopping their
blood by their scarfs, and endeavoring to extricate them-
10 selves from the tumult. The mounted knights, whose
lances had been almost all broken by the fury of the encounter, were now closely engaged with their swords,
shouting their war cries, and exchanging buffets, as if
honor and life depended on the issue of the combat.

15 The tumult was presently increased by the advance
of the second rank on either side, which, acting as a re-
serve, now rushed on to aid their companions. The followers of Brian de Bois-Guilbert shouted, "*Ha! Beau-
Seant! Beau-Seant!*—for the Temple, for the Temple!"
20 The opposite party shouted in answer,—"*Desdichado!
Desdichado!*" which watchword they took from the motto
on their leader's shield.

The champions thus encountering each other with the
utmost fury, and with alternate success the tide of battle
25 seemed to flow now toward the southern, now toward
the northern extremity of the lists, as the one or the other
party prevailed. Meantime the clang of the blows, and
the shouts of the combatants, mixed fearfully with the
sound of the trumpets, and drowned the groans of those
30 who fell and lay rolling defenceless beneath the feet of the
horses. The splendid armor of the combatants was now
defaced with dust and blood, and gave way at every stroke
of the sword and battle-axe. The gay plumage, shorn
from the crests, drifted upon the breeze like snowflakes.
35 All that was beautiful and graceful in the martial array

had disappeared, and what was now visible was only calculated to awake terror or compassion.

Yet such is the force of habit, that not only the vulgar
spectators, who are naturally attracted by sights of hor-
5 ror, but even the ladies of distinction, who crowded the
galleries, saw the conflict with a thrilling interest certainly,
but without a wish to withdraw their eyes from a sight
so terrible. Here and there, indeed, a fair cheek might
turn pale, or a faint scream might be heard, as a lover, a
10 brother, or a husband, was struck from his horse. But, in
general, the ladies around encouraged the combatants, not
only by clapping their hands and waving their veils and
kerchiefs, but even by exclaiming, "Brave lance! Good
sword!" when any successful thrust or blow took place
15 under their observation.

Such being the interest taken by the fair sex in this
bloody game, that of the men is the more easily understood. It showed itself in loud acclamations upon
every change of fortune, while all eyes were so riveted on
20 the lists, that the spectators seemed as if they themselves
had dealt and received the blows which were so freely
bestowed. And between every pause was heard the voice
of the heralds, exclaiming, "Fight on, brave knights! Man
dies, but glory lives!—Fight on;—death is better than de-
25 feat!—Fight on, brave knights!—for bright eyes behold
your deeds!"

Amid the varied fortunes of the combat, the eyes of all
endeavored to discover the leaders of each band, who,
mingling in the thick of the fight, encouraged their com-
30 panions both by voice and example. Both displayed
great feats of gallantry, nor did either Bois-Guilbert or
the Disinherited Knight find in the ranks opposed to them
a champion who could be termed their unquestioned
match. They repeatedly endeavored to single out each
35 other, spurred by mutual animosity, and aware that the

fall of either leader might be considered as decisive of
victory. Such, however, was the crowd and confusion,
that, during the early part of the conflict, their efforts
to meet were unavailing, and they were repeatedly sepa-
5 rated by the eagerness of their followers, each of whom
was anxious to win honor, by measuring his strength
against the leader of the opposite party.

But when the field became thin by the numbers on
either side who had yielded themselves vanquished, had
10 been compelled to the extremity of the lists, or been otherwise rendered incapable of continuing the strife, the
Templar and the Disinherited Knight at length encountered hand to hand, with all the fury that mortal animosity, joined to rivalry of honor, could inspire. Such
15 was the address of each in parrying and striking, that the
spectators broke forth into a unanimous and involuntary
shout, expressive of their delight and admiration.

But at this moment the party of the Disinherited
Knight had the worst; the gigantic arm of Front-de-Bœuf
20 on the one flank, and the ponderous strength of Athelstane on the other, bearing down and dispersing those immediately exposed to them. Finding themselves freed
from their immediate antagonists, it seems to have
occurred to both these knights at the same instant, that
25 they would render the most decisive advantage to their
party, by aiding the Templar in his contest with his rival.
Turning their horses, therefore, at the same moment, the
Norman spurred against the Disinherited Knight on the
one side, and the Saxon on the other. It was utterly im-
30 possible that the object of this unequal and unexpected
assault could have sustained it, had he not been warned
by a general cry from the spectators, who could not but
take interest in one exposed to such disadvantage.

"Beware! beware! Sir Disinherited!" was shouted so
35 universally, that the knight became aware of his danger;

and, striking a full blow at the Templar, he reined back
his steed in the same moment, so as to escape the charge
of Athelstane and Front-de-Bœuf. These knights, therefore, their aim being thus eluded, rushed from opposite
5 sides betwixt the object of their attack and the Templar,
almost running their horses against each other ere they
could stop their career. Recovering their horses, however, and wheeling them round, the whole three pursued
their united purpose of bearing to the earth the Disin-
10 herited Knight.

Nothing could have saved him, except the remarkable
strength and activity of the noble horse which he had
won on the preceding day.

This stood him in the more stead, as the horse of Bois-
15 Guilbert was wounded, and those of Front-de-Bœuf and
Athelstane were both tired with the weight of their gigantic masters, clad in complete armor, and with the preceding exertions of the day. The masterly horsemanship
of the Disinherited Knight, and the activity of the noble
20 animal which he mounted, enabled him for a few minutes
to keep at sword's point his three antagonists, turning and
wheeling with the agility of a hawk upon the wing, keeping his enemies as far separate as he could, and rushing
now against the one, now against the other, dealing sweep-
25 ing blows with his sword, without waiting to receive those
which were aimed at him in return.

But although the lists rang with the applauses of his
dexterity, it was evident that he must at last be over-
powered; and the nobles around Prince John implored
30 him with one voice to throw down his warder, and to save
so brave a knight from the disgrace of being overcome by
odds.

"Not I, by the light of heaven!" answered Prince
John; "this same springal, who conceals his name, and
35 despises our proffered hospitality, hath already gained one

prize, and may now afford to let others have their turn."
As he spoke thus, an unexpected incident changed the
fortune of the day.

There was among the ranks of the Disinherited Knight,
5 a champion in black armor, mounted on a black horse,
large of size, tall, and to all appearance powerful and strong,
like the rider by whom he was mounted. This knight,
who bore on his shield no device of any kind, had hitherto
evinced very little interest in the event of the fight, beat-
10 ing off with seeming ease those combatants who attacked
him, but neither pursuing his advantages, nor himself
assailing any one. In short, he had hitherto acted the
part rather of a spectator than of a party in the tournament, a circumstance which procured him among the
15 spectators the name of "*Le Noir Faineant*," or the Black
Sluggard.

At once this knight seemed to throw aside his apathy,
when he discovered the leader of his party so hard be-
sted; for, setting spurs to his horse, which was quite
20 fresh, he came to his assistance like a thunderbolt, exclaiming, in a voice like a trumpet-call, "*Desdichado*, to
the rescue!" It was high time; for, while the Disinherited
Knight was pressing upon the Templar, Front-de-Bœuf
had got nigh to him with his uplifted sword; but ere the
25 blow could descend, the Sable Knight dealt a stroke on
his head, which, glancing from the polished helmet, lighted
with violence scarcely abated on the "chamfron" of his
steed, and Front-de-Bœuf rolled on the ground, both
horse and man equally stunned by the fury of the blow.
30 "*Le Noir Faineant*" then turned his horse upon Athelstane of Coningsburgh; and his own sword having been
broken in his encounter with Front-de-Bœuf, he wrenched
from the hand of the bulky Saxon the battle-axe which he
wielded, and, like one familiar with the use of the weapon,
35 bestowed him such a blow upon the crest, that Athelstane

also lay senseless on the field. Having achieved this double feat, for which he was the more highly applauded that it was totally unexpected from him, the knight seemed to resume the sluggishness of his character, re-
5 turning calmly to the northern extremity of the lists, leaving his leader to cope as he best could with Brian de Bois-Guilbert. This was no longer a matter of so much difficulty as formerly. The Templar's horse had bled much, and gave way under the shock of the Disinherited
10 Knight's charge. Brian de Bois-Guilbert rolled on the field, encumbered with the stirrup, from which he was unable to draw his foot. His antagonist sprung from horseback, waved his fatal sword over the head of his adversary, and commanded him to yield himself; when
15 Prince John, more moved by the Templar's dangerous situation than he had been by that of his rival, saved him the mortification of confessing himself vanquished, by casting down his warder, and putting an end to the conflict.

It was, indeed, only the relics and embers of the fight
20 which continued to burn; for of the few knights who still continued in the lists, the greater part had, by tacit consent, forborne the conflict for some time, leaving it to be determined by the strife of the leaders.

The squires, who had found it a matter of danger and
25 difficulty to attend their masters during the engagement, now thronged into the lists to pay their dutiful attendance to the wounded, who were removed with the utmost care and attention to the neighboring pavilions, or to the quarters prepared for them in the adjoining village.
30   Thus ended the memorable field of Ashby-de-la-Zouche, one of the most gallantly contested tournaments of that age; for although only four knights, including one who was smothered by the heat of his armor, had died upon the field, yet upwards of thirty were desperately
35 wounded, four or five of whom never recovered. Several

more were disabled for life; and those who escaped best
carried the marks of the conflict to the grave with them.
Hence it is always mentioned in the old records, as the
Gentle and Joyous Passage of Arms of Ashby.

5   It being now the duty of Prince John to name the
knight who had done best, he determined that the honor
of the day remained with the knight whom the popular
voice had termed "*Le Noir Faineant.*"   It was pointed
out to the Prince, in impeachment of this decree, that the
10 victory had been in fact won by the Disinherited Knight,
who, in the course of the day, had overcome six champions with his own hand, and who had finally unhorsed
and struck down the leader of the opposite party.   But
Prince John adhered to his own opinion, on the ground
15 that the Disinherited Knight and his party had lost the
day but for the powerful assistance of the Knight of the
Black Armor, to whom, therefore, he persisted in award-
ing the prize.

    To the surprise of all present, however, the knight
20 thus preferred was nowhere to be found.   He had left the
lists immediately when the conflict ceased, and had been
observed by some spectators to move down one of the
forest glades with the same slow pace and listless and in-
different manner which had procured him the epithet of
25 the Black Sluggard.   After he had been summoned twice
by sound of trumpet, and proclamation of the heralds, it
became necessary to name another to receive the honors
which had been assigned to him.   Prince John had now
no further excuse for resisting the claim of the Disinherited
30 Knight, whom, therefore, he named the champion of the
day.

    Through a field slippery with blood, and encumbered
with broken armor and the bodies of slain and wounded
horses, the marshals of the list again conducted the victor
35 to the foot of Prince John's throne.

"Disinherited Knight," said Prince John, "since by
that title only you will consent to be known to us, we a
second time award to you the honors of this tournament,
and announce to you your right to claim and receive from
5 the hands of the Queen of Love and Beauty, the Chaplet
of Honor which your valor has justly deserved." The
knight bowed low and gracefully, but returned no
answer.

While the trumpets sounded, while the heralds strained
10 their voices in proclaiming honor to the brave and glory
to the victor, while ladies waved their silken kerchiefs and
embroidered veils, and while all ranks joined in a clamor-
ous shout of exultation, the marshals conducted the Disinherited Knight across the lists to the foot of that throne
15 of honor which was occupied by the Lady Rowena.

On the lower step of this throne the champion was
made to kneel down. Indeed, his whole action since the
fight had ended, seemed rather to have been upon the
impulse of those around him rather than from his own
20 free will; and it was observed that he tottered as they
guided him the second time across the lists. Rowena,
descending from her station with a graceful and dignified
step, was about to place the chaplet which she held in her
hand upon the helmet of the champion, when the mar-
25 shals exclaimed with one voice, "It must not be thus—
his head must be bare." The knight muttered faintly a
few words, which were lost in the hollow of his helmet, but
their purport seemed to be a desire that his casque might
not be removed.

30   Whether from love of form, or from curiosity, the marshals paid no attention to his expressions of reluctance,
but unhelmed him by cutting the laces of his casque, and
undoing the fastening of his gorget. When the helmet
was removed, the well-formed, yet sunburned features of a
35 young man of twenty-five were seen, amidst a profusion of

short fair hair. His countenance was as pale as death, and marked in one or two places with streaks of blood.

Rowena had no sooner beheld him than she uttered a faint shriek; but at once summoning up the energy of her
5 disposition, and compelling herself, as it were, to proceed, while her frame yet trembled with the violence of sudden emotion, she placed upon the drooping head of the victor the splendid chaplet which was the destined reward of the day, and pronounced, in a clear and distinct tone, these
10 words: "I bestow on thee this chaplet, Sir Knight, as the meed of valor assigned to this day's victor." Here she paused a moment, and then firmly added, "And upon brows more worthy could a wreath of chivalry never be placed!"

15 The knight stooped his head, and kissed the hand of the lovely Sovereign by whom his valor had been rewarded; and then, sinking yet farther forward, lay prostrate at her feet.

There was a general consternation. Cedric, who had
20 been struck mute by the sudden appearance of his banished son, now rushed forward, as if to separate him from Rowena. But this had been already accomplished by the marshals of the field, who, guessing the cause of Ivanhoe's swoon, had hastened to undo his armor, and found that
25 the head of a lance had penetrated his breastplate, and inflicted a wound in his side.

NOTES AND SUGGESTIONS

"Ivanhoe" is a historical novel. A novel of this type is one that tells a story that is pure fiction but makes use of historical events as a setting for the plot. In regard to minor details, it is not a reason for adverse criticism if the author is not historically accurate.

This story gives a splendid picture of society in England in the 12th century. The enmity between Saxon and Norman is interestingly set forth; the treatment of the Jews is described; the mode of living, the home life, the customs and amusements of the people are all brought out incidental to the story. The impressions made are not all historically correct. For example, King Richard is placed in a far more heroic light than he deserved, but in the main the picture is correct and interesting and instructive. It will amply repay you to read this story in its entirety at home.

1. What is meant by the Age of Chivalry?
2. What were the divisions of society during the feudal times?
3. How did they compel an observance of the laws of chivalry?
4. In this extract, where is that brought out?
5. Compare the form of amusement described in this selection, with some of the modern forms of recreation.

Explanatory Notes

Page 95, line 8—"Knight Templar"—one of a religious and military order first established at Jerusalem in the early part of the 12th century, for the protection of pilgrims and the Holy Sepulcher.

Page 98, line 22—"laissez aller"—a signal to start; literally, "let go."

Page 99, line 18—"Beau-Seant"—was the name of the Templars' banner, which was half black, half white, to intimate that they were candid and fair towards Christians, but black and terrible towards infidels.

Page 103, line 27—"chamfron"—the head armor of a horse.

Suggestions for Home Reading

Scott's "The Talisman"—a story of Richard and the Third Crusade.

Pyle's "Men of Iron"—an interesting account of the training of a youth of the nobility in preparation for knighthood during the feudal ages.

Mitchell's "Hugh Wynne"—a historical novel making use of the Revolutionary period as a background for the story.

ART AND THE BRONCO

BY O. HENRY

O. Henry was the nom-de-plume of William S. Porter, who was born in North Carolina in 1865 and died in New York in 1910. He spent his boyhood on a cattle-ranch in Texas. Later he did newspaper work in the South and then continued that work in New York.

Nearly all of his literary work was done in the form of short stories and sketches of life in the southwest and in New York city. His skill in handling this form gained for him an immediate recognition as a master of short-story writing. His tales are perfectly constructed and told in vigorous picturesque language. In many of his stories, he gives an unexpected turn to the ending, the effect of which is delightful.

OUT of the wilderness had come a painter. Genius, whose coronations alone are democratic, had woven a chaplet of chaparral for the brow of Lonny Briscoe. Art, whose divine expression flows impartially from the finger-

5 tips of a cowboy or a dilettante emperor, had chosen for a medium the Boy Artist of the San Saba. The outcome, seven feet by twelve of besmeared canvas, stood, gilt-framed, in the lobby of the Capitol.

The legislature was in session; the capital city of that

10 great Western state was enjoying the season of activity and profit that the congregation of the solons bestowed. The boarding-houses were corralling the easy dollars of the gamesome law-makers. The greatest state in the West, an empire in area and resources, had arisen and

15 repudiated the old libel of barbarism, law breaking, and bloodshed. Order reigned within her borders. Life and property were as safe there, sir, as anywhere among the corrupt cities of the effete East. Pillow-shams, churches, strawberry feasts and *habeas corpus* flourished. With

20 impunity might the tenderfoot ventilate his "stovepipe" or his theories of culture. The arts and sciences received nurture and subsidy. And, therefore, it behooved the legislature of this great state to make appropriation for the purchase of Lonny Briscoe's immortal painting.

25 Rarely has the San Saba country contributed to the spread of the fine arts. Its sons have excelled in the soldier graces, in the throw of the lariat, the manipulation of the esteemed .45, the intrepidity of the one-card draw,

and the nocturnal stimulation of towns from undue leth-
argy; but, hitherto, it had not been famed as a stronghold
of æsthetics. Lonny Briscoe's brush had removed that
disability. Here, among the limestone rocks, the succu-
5 lent cactus, and the drought-parched grass of that arid
valley, had been born the Boy Artist. Why he came to
woo art is beyond postulation. Beyond doubt, some
spore of the afflatus must have sprung up within him in
spite of the desert soil of San Saba. The tricksy spirit of
10 creation must have incited him to attempted expression
and then have sat hilarious among the white-hot sands of
the valley, watching its mischievous work. For Lonny's
picture, viewed as a thing of art, was something to have
driven away dull care from the bosoms of the critics.
15   The painting—one might almost say panorama—was
designed to portray a typical Western scene, interest cul-
minating in a central animal figure, that of a stampeding
steer, life-size, wild-eyed, fiery, breaking away in a mad
rush from the herd that, close-ridden by a typical cow-
20 puncher, occupied a position somewhat in the right background of the picture. The landscape presented fitting
and faithful accessories. Chaparral, mesquit and pear
were distributed in just proportions. A Spanish dagger-
plant, with its waxen blossoms in a creamy aggregation
25 as large as a water-bucket, contributed floral beauty and
variety. The distance was undulating prairie, bisected
by stretches of the intermittent streams peculiar to the
region lined with the rich green of live-oak and water-elm.
A richly mottled rattlesnake lay coiled beneath a pale
30 green clump of prickly pear in the foreground. A third
of the canvas was ultramarine and lake white—the typical
Western sky and the flying clouds, rainless and feathery.
     Between two plastered pillars in the commodious hall-
way near the door of the chamber of representatives stood
35 the painting. Citizens and lawmakers passed there by

twos and groups and sometimes crowds to gaze upon it.
Many—perhaps a majority of them—had lived the prairie
life and recalled easily the familiar scene. Old cattlemen
stood, reminiscent and candidly pleased, chatting with
5 brothers of former camps and trails of the days it brought
back to mind. Art critics were few in the town, and there
was heard none of that jargon of color, perspective, and
feeling such as the East loves to use as a curb and a rod
to the pretensions of the artist. 'Twas a great picture,
10 most of them agreed, admiring the gilt frame—larger than
any they had ever seen.

Senator Kinney was the picture's champion and
sponsor. It was he who so often stepped forward and
asserted, with the voice of a bronco-buster, that it would
15 be a lasting blot, sir, upon the name of this great state if
it should decline to recognize in a proper manner the
genius that had so brilliantly transferred to imperishable
canvas a scene so typical of the great sources of our
state's wealth and prosperity, land and—er—live-stock.
20   Senator Kinney represented a section of the state in
the extreme west—four hundred miles from the San Saba
country—but the true lover of art is not limited by metes
and bounds. Nor was Senator Mullens, representing the
San Saba country, lukewarm in his belief that the state
25 should purchase the painting of his constituent. He was
advised that the San Saba country was unanimous in its
admiration of the great painting by one of its own deni-
zens. Hundreds of connoisseurs had straddled their
broncos and ridden miles to view it before its removal to
30 the capital. Senator Mullens desired reelection, and he
knew the importance of the San Saba vote. He also
knew that with the help of Senator Kinney—who was a
power in the legislature—the thing could be put through.
Now, Senator Kinney had an irrigation bill that he wanted
35 passed for the benefit of his own section, and he knew

Senator Mullens could render him valuable aid and information, the San Saba country already enjoying the benefits of similar legislation. With these interests happily dovetailed, wonder at the sudden interest in art at
5 the state capital must, necessarily, be small. Few artists have uncovered their first picture to the world under happier auspices than did Lonny Briscoe.

Senators Kinney and Mullens came to an understanding in the matter of irrigation and art while partaking of
10 long drinks in the café of the Empire Hotel.

"H'm!" said Senator Kinney, "I don't know. I'm no art critic, but it seems to me the thing won't work. It looks like the worst kind of a chromo to me. I don't want to cast any reflections upon the artistic talent of
15 your constituent, Senator, but I, myself, wouldn't give six bits for the picture—without the frame. How are you going to cram a thing like that down the throat of a legislature that kicks about a little item in the expense bill of six hundred and eighty-one dollars for rubber erasers for
20 only one term? It's wasting time. I'd like to help you, Mullens, but they'd laugh us out of the Senate chamber if we were to try it."

"But you don't get the point," said Senator Mullens, in his deliberate tones, tapping Kinney's glass with his
25 long forefinger. "I have my own doubts as to what the picture is intended to represent, a bull-fight or a Japanese allegory, but I want this legislature to make an appropriation to purchase. Of course, the subject of the picture should have been in the state historical line, but it's too
30 late to have the paint scraped off and changed. The state won't miss the money and the picture can be stowed away in a lumber-room where it won't annoy anyone. Now, here's the point to work on, leaving art to look after itself—the chap that painted the picture is the grandson
35 of Lucien Briscoe."

"Say it again," said Kinney, leaning his head thought-
fully. "Of the old, original Lucien Briscoe?"

"Of him. 'The man who,' you know. The man who
carved the state out of the wilderness. The man who
5 settled the Indians. The man who cleaned out the horse
thieves. The man who refused the crown. The state's
favorite son. Do you see the point now?"

"Wrap up the picture," said Kinney. "It's as good
as sold. Why didn't you say that at first, instead of
10 philandering along about art? I'll resign my seat in the
Senate and go back to chain-carrying for the county sur-
veyor the day I can't make this state buy a picture calci-
mined by a grandson of Lucien Briscoe. Did you ever
hear of a special appropriation for the purchase of a home
15 for the daughter of One-Eyed Smothers? Well, that went
through like a motion to adjourn, and old One-Eyed never
killed half as many Indians as Briscoe did. About what
figure had you and the calciminer agreed upon to sandbag
the treasury for?"

20 "I thought," said Mullens, "that maybe five hundred——"

"Five hundred!" interrupted Kinney, as he hammered
on his glass with a lead pencil and looked around for a
waiter. "Only five hundred for a red steer on the hoof
25 delivered by a grandson of Lucien Briscoe! Where's your
state pride, man? Two thousand is what it'll be. You'll
introduce the bill and I'll get up on the floor of the Senate
and wave the scalp of every Indian old Lucien ever mur-
dered. Let's see, there was something else proud and
30 foolish he did, wasn't there? Oh, yes; he declined all
emoluments and benefits he was entitled to. Refused his
head-right and veteran donation certificates. Could have
been governor, but wouldn't. Declined a pension. Now's
the state's chance to pay up. It'll have to take the pic-
35 ture, but then it deserves some punishment for keeping

the Briscoe family waiting so long. We'll bring this
thing up about the middle of the month, after the tax bill
is settled.   Now, Mullens, you send over, as soon as you
can, and get me the figures on the cost of those irrigation
5 ditches and the statistics about the increased production
per acre.   I'm going to need you when that bill of mine
comes up.   I reckon we'll be able to pull along pretty well
together this session and maybe others to come, eh,
Senator?"

10   Thus did Fortune elect to smile upon the Boy Artist of
the San Saba.   Fate had already done her share when she
arranged his atoms in the cosmogony of creation as the
grandson of Lucien Briscoe.

The original Briscoe had been a pioneer both as to
15 territorial occupation and in certain acts prompted by a
great and simple heart.   He had been one of the first
settlers and crusaders against the wild forces of nature,
the savage and the shallow politician.   His name and
memory were revered equally with any upon the list com-
20 prising Houston, Boone, Crockett, Clark, and Green.   He
had lived simply, independently, and unvexed by ambi-
tion.   Even a less shrewd man than Senator Kinney
could have prophesied that his state would hasten to honor
and reward his grandson, come out of the chaparral at
25 even so late a day.

And so, before the great picture by the door of the
chamber of representatives at frequent times for many
days could be found the breezy, robust form of Senator
Kinney and be heard his clarion voice reciting the past
30 deeds of Lucien Briscoe in connection with the handiwork
of his grandson.   Senator Mullens' work was more subdued in sight and sound, but directed along identical
lines.

Then, as the day for the introduction of the bill for
35 appropriation draws nigh, up from the San Saba country

rides Lonny Briscoe and a loyal lobby of cowpunchers, bronco-back, to boost the cause of art and glorify the name of friendship, for Lonny is one of them, a knight of the stirrup and chaparreras, as handy with the lariat and
5 .45 as he is with brush and palette.

On a March afternoon the lobby dashed, with a whoop, into town. The cowpunchers had adjusted their garb suitably from that prescribed for the range to the more conventional requirements of town. They had conceded
10 their leather chaparreras and transferred their six-shooters and belts from their persons to the horns of their saddles. Among them rode Lonny, a youth of twenty-three, brown, solemn-faced, ingenuous, bow-legged, reticent, bestriding Hot Tamales, the most sagacious cow pony west of the
15 Mississippi. Senator Mullens had informed him of the bright prospects of the situation; had even mentioned— so great was his confidence in the capable Kinney—the price that the state would, in all likelihood, pay. It seemed to Lonny that fame and fortune were in his hands.
20 Certainly, a spark of the divine fire was in the little brown centaur's breast, for he was counting the two thousand dollars as but a means to future development of his talent. Some day he would paint a picture even greater than this —one, say, twelve feet by twenty, full of scope and atmos-
25 phere and action.

During the three days that yet intervened before the coming of the date fixed for the introduction of the bill, the centaur lobby did valiant service. Coatless, spurred, weather-tanned, full of enthusiasm expressed in bizarre
30 terms, they loafed in front of the painting with tireless zeal. Reasoning not unshrewdly, they estimated that their comments upon its fidelity to nature would be received as expert evidence. Loudly they praised the skill of the painter whenever there were ears near to which
35 such evidence might be profitably addressed. Lem Perry,

the leader of the claque, had a somewhat set speech, being uninventive in the construction of new phrases.

"Look at that two-year-old, now," he would say, waving a cinnamon-brown hand toward the salient point of
5 the picture. "Why, dang my hide, the critter's alive. I can jest hear him, 'lumpety-lump,' a-cuttin' away from the herd, pretendin' he's skeered. He's a mean scamp, that there steer. Look at his eyes a-wallin' and his tail a-wavin'. He's true and nat'ral to life. He's jest han-
10 kerin' fur a cow pony to round him up and send him scootin' back to the bunch. Dang my hide! jest look at that tail of his a-wavin'. Never knowed a steer to wave his tail any other way, dang my hide ef I did."

Jud Shelby, while admitting the excellence of the steer,
15 resolutely confined himself to open admiration of the landscape, to the end that the entire picture receive its meed of praise.

"That piece of range," he declared, "is a dead ringer for Dead Hoss Valley. Same grass, same lay of the land,
20 same old Whipperwill Creek skallyhootin' in and out of them motts of timber. Them buzzards on the left is circlin' 'round over Sam Kildrake's old paint hoss that killed hisself over-drinkin' on a hot day. You can't see the hoss for that mott of ellums on the creek, but he's
25 thar. Anybody that was goin' to look for Dead Hoss Valley and come across this picture, why, he'd jest light off'n his bronco and hunt a place to camp."

Skinny Rogers, wedded to comedy, conceived a complimentary little piece of acting that never failed to make
30 an impression. Edging quite near to the picture, he would suddenly, at favorable moments emit a piercing and awful "Yi-yi!" leap high and away, coming down with a great stamp of heels and whirring of rowels upon the stone-flagged floor.

35   "Jeeming Christopher!"—so ran his lines—"thought

that rattler was a gin-u-ine one. Ding baste my skin if
I didn't. Seemed to me I heard him rattle. Look at the
blamed, unconverted insect a-layin' under that pear.
Little more, and somebody would a-been snake-bit."

5   With these artful dodges, contributed by Lonny's
faithful coterie, with the sonorous Kinney perpetually
sounding the picture's merits, and with the solvent pres-
tige of the pioneer Briscoe covering it like a precious var-
nish, it seemed that the San Saba country could not fail
10 to add a reputation as an art center to its well-known
superiority in steer-roping contests and achievements
with the precarious busted flush. Thus was created for
the picture an atmosphere, due rather to externals than
to the artist's brush, but through it the people seemed to
15 gaze with more of admiration. There was a magic in the
name of Briscoe that counted high against faulty tech-
nique and crude coloring. The old Indian fighter and
wolf slayer would have smiled grimly in his happy hunting grounds had he known that his dilettante ghost was
20 thus figuring as an art patron two generations after his
uninspired existence.

Came the day when the Senate was expected to pass
the bill of Senator Mullens appropriating two thousand
dollars for the purchase of the picture. The gallery of
25 the Senate chamber was early preempted by Lonny and
the San Saba lobby. In the front row of chairs they sat,
wild-haired, self-conscious, jingling, creaking, and rattling,
subdued by the majesty of the council hall.

The bill was introduced, went to the second reading,
30 and then Senator Mullens spoke for it dryly, tediously,
and at length. Senator Kinney then arose, and the wel-
kin seized the bellrope preparatory to ringing. Oratory
was at that time a living thing; the world had not quite
come to measure its questions by geometry and the multi-
35 plication table. It was the day of the silver tongue, the

sweeping gesture, the decorative apostrophe, the moving peroration.

The Senator spoke. The San Saba contingent sat, breathing hard, in the gallery, its disordered hair hanging
5 down to its eyes, its sixteen-ounce hats shifted restlessly from knee to knee. Below, the distinguished Senators either lounged at their desks with the abandon of proven statesmanship or maintained correct attitudes indicative of a first term.

10 Senator Kinney spoke for an hour. History was his theme—history mitigated by patriotism and sentiment. He referred casually to the picture in the outer hall—it was unnecessary, he said, to dilate upon its merits—the Senators had seen for themselves. The painter of the
15 picture was the grandson of Lucien Briscoe. Then came the word-pictures of Briscoe's life set forth in thrilling colors. His rude and venturesome life, his simple-minded love for the commonwealth he helped to upbuild, his contempt for rewards and praise, his extreme and sturdy
20 independence, and the great service he had rendered the state. The subject of the oration was Lucien Briscoe; the painting stood in the background serving simply as a means, now happily brought forward, through which the state might bestow a tardy recompense upon the descend-
25 ant of its favorite son. Frequent enthusiastic applause from the Senators testified to the well reception of the sentiment.

The bill passed without an opposing vote. To-morrow it would be taken up by the House. Already was it
30 fixed to glide through that body on rubber tires. Blandford, Grayson and Plummer, all wheel-horses and orators, and provided with plentiful memoranda concerning the deeds of pioneer Briscoe, had agreed to furnish the motive power.

35 The San Saba lobby and its *protégé* stumbled awk-

wardly down the stairs and out into the Capitol yard.
Then they herded closely and gave one yell of triumph.
But one of them—Buck-kneed Summers it was—hit the
key with the thoughtful remark:

5   "She cut the mustard," he said, "all right. I reckon
they're goin' to buy Lon's steer. I ain't right much on
the parlyment'ry, but I gather that's what the signs
added up. But she seems to me, Lonny, the argyment
ran principal to grandfather, instead of paint. It's rea-
10 sonable calculatin' that you want to be glad you got the
Briscoe brand on you, my son."

That remark clinched in Lonny's mind an unpleasant,
vague suspicion to the same effect. His reticence increased, and he gathered grass from the ground, chewing
15 it pensively. The picture as a picture had been humiliatingly absent from the Senator's arguments. The
painter had been held up as a grandson, pure and simple.
While this was gratifying on certain lines, it made art look
little and slab-sided. The Boy Artist was thinking.

20   The hotel Lonny stopped at was near the Capitol.
It was near to the one o'clock dinner hour when the appropriation had been passed by the Senate. The hotel
clerk told Lonny that a famous artist from New York had
arrived in town that day and was in the hotel. He was
25 on his way westward to New Mexico to study the effect
of sunlight upon the ancient walls of the Zunis. Modern
stone reflects light. Those ancient building materials
absorb it. The artist wanted this effect in a picture he
was painting and was traveling two thousand miles to
30 get it.

Lonny sought this man out after dinner and told his
story. The artist was an unhealthy man, kept alive by
genius and indifference to life. He went with Lonny to
the Capitol and stood there before the picture. The
35 artist pulled his beard and looked unhappy.

"Should like to have your sentiments," said Lonny, "just as they run out of the pen."

"It's the way they'll come," said the painter man. "I took three different kinds of medicine before dinner—
5 by the tablespoonful. The taste still lingers. I am primed for telling the truth. You want to know if the picture is, or if it isn't?"

"Right," said Lonny. "Is it wool or cotton? Should I paint some more or cut it out and ride herd a-plenty?"

10   "I heard rumor during pie," said the artist, "that the state is about to pay you two thousand dollars for this picture."

"It's passed the Senate," said Lonny, "and the House rounds it up to-morrow."

15   "That's lucky," said the pale man. "Do you carry a rabbit's foot?"

"No," said Lonny, "but it seems I had a grandfather. He's considerable mixed up in the color scheme. It took me a year to paint that picture. Is she entirely awful or
20 not? Some says now, that that steer's tail ain't badly drawed. They think it is proportioned nice. Tell me."

The artist glanced at Lonny's wiry figure and nut-brown skin. Something stirred him to a passing irritation.

25   "For Art's sake, son," he said, fractiously, "don't spend any more money for paint. It isn't a picture at all. It's a gun. You hold up the state with it, if you like, and get your two thousand, but don't get in front of any more canvas. Live under it. Buy a couple of hun-
30 dred ponies with the money—I'm told they are that cheap —and ride, ride, ride. Fill your lungs and eat and sleep and be happy. No more pictures. You look healthy. That's genius. Cultivate it." He looked at his watch. "Twenty minutes to three. Four capsules and one tab-
35 let at three. That's all you wanted to know, isn't it?"

At three o'clock the cowpunchers rode up for Lonny, bringing Hot Tamales, saddled. Traditions must be observed. To celebrate the passage of the bill by the Senate the gang must ride wildly through the town, 5 creating uproar and excitement. Liquor must be partaken of, the suburbs shot up, and the glory of the San Saba country vociferously proclaimed. A part of the programme had been carried out in the saloons on the way up.

10 Lonny mounted Hot Tamales, the accomplished little beast prancing with fire and intelligence. He was glad to feel Lonny's bow-legged grip against his ribs again. Lonny was his friend, and he was willing to do things for him.

15 "Come on, boys," said Lonny, urging Hot Tamales into a gallop with his knees. With a whoop the inspired lobby tore after him through the dust. Lonny led his cohorts straight for the Capitol. With a wild yell, the gang indorsed his now evident attention of riding into it. 20 Hooray for San Saba!

Up six broad, limestone steps clattered the broncos of the cowpunchers. Into the resounding hallway they pattered, scattering in dismay those passing on foot. Lonny, in the lead, shoved Hot Tamales direct for the 25 great picture. At that hour a downpouring, soft light from the second story windows bathed the big canvas. Against the darker background of the hall the painting stood out with valuable effect. In spite of the defects of the art you could almost fancy that you gazed out upon 30 a landscape. You might well flinch a step from the convincing figure of the life-size steer stampeding across the grass. Perhaps it thus seemed to Hot Tamales. The scene was in his line. Perhaps he only obeyed the will of his rider. His ears pricked up; he snorted. Lonny 35 leaned forward in the saddle and elevated his elbows,

winglike.   Thus signals the cowpuncher to his steed to
launch himself full speed ahead.   Did Hot Tamales fancy
he saw a steer, red and cavorting, that should be headed
off and driven back to herd?   There was a fierce clatter
5 of hoofs, a rush, a gathering of steely-flanked muscles, a
leap to the jerk of the bridle rein, and Hot Tamales, with
Lonny bending low in the saddle to dodge the top of the
frame, ripped through the great canvas like a shell from
a mortar, leaving the cloth hanging in ragged shreds
10 about a monstrous hole.

Quickly, Lonny pulled up his pony, and rounded the
pillars.   Spectators came running, too astounded to add
speech to the commotion.   The sergeant-at-arms of the
House came forth, frowned, looked ominous, and then
15 grinned.   Many of the legislators crowded out to observe
the tumult.   Lonny's cowpunchers were striken to silent
horror by his mad deed.

Senator Kinney happened to be among the earliest to
emerge.   Before he could speak Lonny leaned in his sad-
20 dle as Hot Tamales pranced, pointed his quirt at the
Senator, and said, calmly:

"That was a fine speech you made to-day, mister, but
you might as well let up on that 'propriation business.   I
ain't askin' the state to give me nothin'.   I thought I had
25 a picture to sell to it, but it wasn't one.   You said a heap
of things about Grandfather Briscoe that makes me kind
of proud I'm his grandson.   Well, the Briscoe's ain't
takin' presents from the state yet.   Anybody can have
the frame that wants it.   Hit her up, boys."

30   Away scuttled the San Saba delegation out of the hall,
down the steps, along the dusty street.

Half way to the San Saba country they camped that
night.   At bedtime Lonny stole away from the campfire
and sought Hot Tamales, placidly eating grass at the end
35 of his stake rope.   Lonny hung upon his neck, and his art

aspirations went forth forever in one long, regretful sigh. But as he thus made renunciation his breath formed a word or two.

"You was the only one, Tamales, what seen anything
5 in it. It did look like a steer, didn't it, old hoss?"

NOTES AND SUGGESTIONS

Try to find out from your study of this selection, how the author creates the proper atmosphere for his story. To do this, point out any of the characteristics of the country and the people of the ranches of the Southwest, brought out incidentally in this story. An author's ability to do this sort of thing without interrupting the action of his story adds greatly to the effectiveness of the tale.

Note carefully the construction of this story.

The first group of paragraphs has to do with the picture.

1. In these paragraphs, what impression of the painting does the author give us?

2. From the description in the fourth paragraph, try, in your imagination, to see the picture. Describe it, in your own way.

3. a. What do the cattlemen think of it?

    b. Explain the reasons for their opinions.

    c. Why does the writer tell us that there were few art critics in town?

The second group of paragraphs discloses why the picture is at the State Capitol.

4. a. Why did Senator Kinney want the state to buy the picture?

    b. What was the reason for Senator Mullens' interest?

5. In the sixth paragraph, there is no direct description of Senator Kinney. From what it says there, however, what can you tell about his character and mannerisms?

The next group of three paragraphs tells of Lucien Briscoe.

6. What made Senator Kinney think that he could succeed in making the Legislature buy the picture?

7. In your own words, describe Lucien Briscoe.

The next group of paragraphs tells of the arrival of Lonny's friends to act as a lobby.

    a. What is a lobby?

    b. How does this lobby attempt to influence opinion concerning the picture?

c. What does Lem Perry say about the picture? Jud Selby? Skinny Rogers?

d. What impression does the author make on you by the introduction of these three characters?

The next paragraph concerns itself with the passage of the bill.

8. a. What is the effect on Lonny of Senator Kinney's speech?

b. What confirms the suspicions that have been aroused?

The next paragraphs have to do with the art critic.

9. a. Why is the critic necessary to the story?

b. Describe him.

The next paragraph tells of the final scene at the Capitol.

10. Point out the climax of the story.

11. Why did Lonny destroy the picture?

12. Compare Lonny with his grandfather, Lucien Briscoe. What traits of character are common to both?

13. What is the effect of the closing sentence of the story?

Explanatory Notes

Page 109, line 3—"chaparral"—a thicket of low evergreen oaks.

Page 109, line 19—"habeas corpus"—in law, a writ having for its purpose the bringing of a person before the court.

Page 110, line 8—"spore of the afflatus"—a germ of divine inspiration.

Page 110, line 22—"mesquit"—a rich native grass in Western Texas, so-called from its growing in company with the mesquit tree.

Page 114, line 20—"Houston"—

Sam Houston was born in Virginia in 1793. He was commander-in-chief of the Texan forces during their struggle for independence.

"Boone"—Daniel Boone was born in Pennsylvania in 1735. He was one of the pioneers in the settlement of Kentucky. He was a famous Indian fighter.

"Crockett"—1786; an American pioneer and politician.

"Clark"—1770; an explorer. At one time governor of the province of Louisiana.

Suggestions for Home Reading

Churchill's "The Crossing"—an accurate, instructive and interesting account of the early days of Kentucky.

White's "The Blazed Trail"—a story of the lumber regions of Michigan, a stirring tale of primitive life.

Monroe's "Dorymates"—a story of the New England whalers.

THE FOOTBALL GAME
(From "The Varmint")

BY OWEN JOHNSON

OWEN JOHNSON, the author of this story, is alive at the present time. He has done newspaper and magazine work and is a novelist and dramatist of distinction. He has written a number of short stories of the school life at Lawrenceville. These have been collected and published under the following titles: "The Prodigious Hickey," "The Tennessee Shad" and the "Humming Bird." He has written one story of college life, "Stover at Yale." All of these stories are characterized by a deep and sympathetic understanding of boys. They compare favorably with the classics of school life, the "Tom Brown" stories. The Johnson stories are more likely to interest the boys and girls of to-day because they deal with a system that is more readily understood by them.

The extract given here is taken from the long story of Lawrenceville school life, "The Varmint." In this story the author traces the career of "Dink" Stover from his entrance as an obstreperous freshman to its close. In a very interesting way we are shown how the various influences work on the pupils for good and evil. It is to be hoped that you will read the complete story at home.

SATURDAY came all too soon and with it the arrival of the stocky Andover eleven. Dink dressed and went slowly across the campus—every step seemed an effort. Everywhere was an air of seriousness and apprehension,
5 strangely contrasted to the gay ferment that usually announced a big game. He felt a hundred eyes on him as he went and knew what was in every one's mind. What would happen when Ned Banks would have to retire and he, little Dink Stover, weighing one hundred and thirty-
10 eight, would have to go forth to stand at the end of the line. And because Stover had learned the lesson of football, the sacrifice for an idea, he too felt not fear but a sort of despair that the hopes of the great school would have

to rest upon him, little Dink Stover, who weighed only
one hundred and thirty-eight pounds.

He went quietly to the Upper, his eyes on the ground
like a guilty man, picking his way through the crowds of
5 Fifth Formers, who watched him pass with critical looks,
and up the heavy stairs to Garry Cockrell's room, where
the team sat quietly listening to final instructions. He
took his seat silently in an obscure corner, studying the
stern faces about him, hearing nothing of Mr. Ware's
10 staccato periods, his eyes irresistibly drawn to his captain, wondering how suddenly older he looked and
grave.

By his side Ned Banks was listening stolidly and
Charlie De Soto, twisting a paper-weight in his nervous
15 fingers, fidgeting on his chair with the longing for the
fray.

"That's all," said the low voice of Garry Cockrell.
"You know what you have to do. Go down to Charlie's
room; I want a few words with Stover."

20   They went sternly and quickly, Mr. Ware with them.
Dink was alone, standing stiff and straight, his heart
thumping violently, waiting for his captain to speak.

"How do you feel?"

"I'm ready, sir."

25   "I don't know when you'll get in the game—probably
before the first half is over," said Cockrell slowly. "We're
going to put up to you a pretty hard proposition, youngster." He came nearer, laying his hand on Stover's
shoulder. "I'm not going to talk nerve to you, young
30 bulldog, I don't need to. I've watched you and I know
the stuff that's in you."

"Thank you, sir."

"Not but what you'll need it—more than you've ever
needed it before. You've no right in this game."

35   "I know it, sir."

"Tough McCarty won't be able to help you out much. He's got the toughest man in the line. Everything's coming at you, my boy, and you've got to stand it off, somehow. Now, listen once more. It's a game for the
5 long head, for the cool head. You've got to think quicker, you've got to outthink every man on the field and you can do it. And remember this; no matter what happens never let up—get your man back of the line if you can, get him twenty-five yards beyond you, get him on the one-
10 yard line,—but get him!"

"Yes, sir."

"And now one thing more. There's all sorts of ways you can play the game. You can charge in like a bull and kill yourself off in ten minutes, but that won't do.
15 You can go in and make grandstand plays and get carried off the field, but that won't do. My boy, you've got to last out the game."

"I see, sir."

"Remember there's a bigger thing than yourself you're
20 fighting for, Stover—it's the school, the old school. Now, when you're on the side-lines don't lose any time; watch your men, find out their tricks, see if they look up or change their footing when they start for an end run. Everything is going to count. Now, come on."

25 They joined the eleven below and presently, in a compact body, went out and through Memorial and the chapel, where suddenly the field appeared and a great roar went up from the school.

"All ready," said the captain.

30 They broke into a trot and swept up to the cheering mass. Dink remembered seeing the Tennessee Shad, in his shirt sleeves, frantically leading the school and thinking how funny he looked. Then some one pulled a blanket over him and he was camped among the substi-
35 tutes, peering out at the gridiron where already the two

elevens were sweeping back and forth in vigorous signal drill.

He looked eagerly at the Andover eleven. They were big, rangy fellows and their team worked with a precision
5 and machine-like rush that the red and black team did not have.

"Trouble with us is," said the voice of Fatty Harris, at his elbow, "our team's never gotten together. The fellows would rather slug each other than the enemy."
10   "Gee, that fellow at tackle is a monster," said Dink, picking out McCarty's opponent.

"Look at Turkey Reiter and the Waladoo Bird," continued Fatty Harris. "Bad blood! And there's Tough McCarty and King Lentz. We're not together, I tell
15 you! We're hanging apart!"

"Lord, will they ever begin!" said Dink, blowing on his hands that had suddenly gone limp and clammy.

"We've won the toss," said another voice. "There's a big wind; we'll take sides."
20   "Andover's kick-off," said Fatty Harris.

Stover sunk his head in his blanket, waiting for the awful moment to end. Then a whistle piped and he raised his head again. The ball had landed short, into the arms of Butcher Stevens, who plunged ahead for a
25 slight gain and went down under a shock of blue jerseys.

Stover felt the warm blood return, the sinking feeling in the pit of his stomach left him; he felt amazed, a great calm settling over him, as though he had jumped from out his own body.
30   "If Flash Condit can once get loose," he said quietly, "he'll score. They ought to try a dash through tackle before the others warm up. Good!"

As if in obedience to his thought Flash Condit came rushing through the line, between end and
35 tackle, but the Andover left halfback, who was alert,

caught him and brought him to the ground after a gain
of ten yards.

"Pretty fast, that chap," thought Dink. "Too bad,
Flash was almost clear."

5 "Who tackled him?" asked Fatty Harris.

"Goodhue," came the answer from somewhere.
"They say he runs the hundred in ten and a fifth."

The next try was not so fortunate, the blue line
charged quicker and stopped Cheyenne Baxter without
10 a gain. Charlie De Soto tried a quarter-back run and
some one broke through between the Waladoo Bird and
Turkey Reiter.

"Not together—not together," said the dismal voice
of Fatty Harris.

15 The signal was given for a punt and the ball lifted in
the air went soaring down the field on the force of the
wind. It was too long a punt for the ends to cover, and
the Andover back with a good start came twisting
through the territory of Ned Banks who had been
20 blocked off by his opponent.

"Watch that Andover end, Stover," said Mr. Ware.
"Study out his methods."

"All right, sir," said Dink, who had watched no one
else.

25 He waited breathless for the first shock of the Andover
attack. It came with a rush, compact and solid, and
swept back the Lawrenceville left side for a good eight
yards.

"Good-by!" said Harris in a whisper.

30 Dink began to whistle, moving down the field, watching the backs. Another machine-like advance and another big gain succeeded.

"They'll wake up," said Dink solemnly to himself.
"They'll stop 'em in a minute."

35 But they did not stop. Rush by rush, irresistibly the

blue left their own territory and passed the forty-five
yard line of Lawrenceville. Then a fumble occurred and
the ball went again with the gale far out of danger, over
the heads of the Andover backs who had misjudged its
5 treacherous course.

"Lucky we've got the wind," said Dink, calm, amid
the roaring cheers about him. "Gee, that Andover
attack's going to be hard to stop. Banks is beginning to
limp."

10   The blue, after a few quick advances, formed and
swept out toward Garry Cockrell's end.

"Three yards lost," said Dink grimly. "They won't
try him often. Funny they're not onto Banks. Lord,
how they can gain through the center of the line. First
15 down again." Substitute and coach, the frantic school,
alumni over from Princeton, kept up a constant storm of
shouts and entreaties:

"Oh, get together!"

"Throw 'em back!"

20   "Hold 'em!"

"First down again!"

"Hold 'em, Lawrenceville!"

"Don't let them carry it seventy yards!"

"Get the jump!"

25   "There they go again!"

"Ten yards around Banks!"

Stover alone, squatting opposite the line of play,
moving as it moved, coldly critical, studied each individuality.

30   "Funny nervous little tricks that Goodhue's got—
blows on his hands—does that mean he takes the ball?
No, all a bluff. What's he do when he does take it?
Quiet and looks at the ground. When he doesn't take
it he tries to pretend he does. I'll tuck that away. He's
35 my man. Seems to switch in just as the interference

strikes the end about ten feet beyond tackle, running low—
Banks is playing too high; better, perhaps, to run in on
'em now and then before they get started. There's going to be trouble there in a minute. The fellows aren't
5 up on their toes yet—what is the matter, anyhow?
Tough's getting boxed right along, he ought to play out
further, I should think. Hello, some one fumbled again.
Who's got it? Looks like Garry. No, they recovered it
themselves—no, they didn't. Lord, what a butter-fingered
10 lot; why doesn't he get it? He has—Charlie De Soto—
clear field—can he make it?—He ought to—where's that
Goodhue?—Looks like a safe lead; he'll make the twenty-
yard line at least—yes, fully that, if he doesn't stumble
—there's that Goodhue now—some one ought to block
15 him off—good work—that's it—that makes the touchdown—lucky—very lucky!''

Some one hit him a terrific clap on the shoulder. He
looked up in surprise to behold Fatty Harris dancing
about like a crazed man. The air seemed all arms, hats
20 were rising like startled coveys of birds. Some one flung
his arms around him and hugged him. He flung him off
almost indignantly. What were they thinking of—that
was only one touchdown—four points—what was that
against that blue team and the wind at their backs, too.
25 One touchdown wasn't going to win the game.

"Why do they get so excited?" said Dink Stover to
John Stover, watching deliberately the ball soaring be-
tween the goal posts; "6 to 0—they think it's all over.
Now's the rub.''

30 Mr. Ware passed near him. He was quiet, too, seeing
far ahead.

"Better keep warmed up, Stover," he said.

"Biting his nails, that's a funny trick for a master,"
thought Dink. "He oughtn't to be nervous. That
35 doesn't do any good."

The shouts of exultation were soon hushed; with the advantage of the wind the game quickly assumed a different complexion. Andover had found the weak end and sent play after play at Banks, driving him back for
5 long advances.

"Take off your sweater," said Mr. Ware.

Dink flung it off, running up and down the side-lines, springing from his toes.

"Why don't they take him out?" he thought angrily,
10 with almost a hatred of the fellow who was fighting it out in vain. "Can't they see it? Ten yards more, oh, Lord! This ends it."

With a final rush the Andover interference swung at Banks, brushing him aside and swept over the remaining
15 fifteen yards for the touchdown. A minute later the goal was kicked and the elevens again changed sides. The suddenness with which the score had been tied impressed every one—the school team seemed to have no defense against the well-massed attacks of the opponents.
20   "Holes as big as a house," said Fatty Harris. "Asleep! They're all asleep!"

Dink, pacing up and down, waited the word from Mr. Ware, rebelling because it did not come.

Again the scrimmage began, a short advance from the
25 loosely-knit school eleven, a long punt with the wind and then a quick, business-like line-up of the blue team and another rush at the vulnerable end.

"Ten yards more; oh, it's giving it away!" said Fatty Harris.
30   Stover knelt and tried his shoe laces and rising, tightened his belt.

"I'll be out there in a moment," he said to himself.

Another gain at Banks' end, and suddenly from the elevens across the field the figure of the captain rose and
35 waved a signal.

"Go in, Stover," said Mr. Ware.

He ran out across the long stretch to where the players were moving restlessly, their clothes flinging out clouds of steam. Back of him something was roaring, cheering
5 for him, perhaps, hoping against hope.

Then he was in the midst of the contestants, Garry Cockrell's arm about his shoulders, whispering something in his ear about keeping cool, breaking up interference if he couldn't get his man, following up the play. He went
10 to his position, noticing the sullen expressions of his team-mates, angry with the consciousness that they were not doing their best. Then taking his stand beyond Tough McCarty, he saw the Andover quarter and the backs turn and study him curiously. He noticed the halfback
15 nearest him, a stocky, close-cropped, red-haired fellow, with brawny arms under his rolled-up jersey, whose duty it would be to send him rolling on the first rush.

"All ready?" cried the voice of the umpire. "First down."
20 The whistle blew, the two lines strained opposite each other. Stover knew what the play would be—there was no question of that. Fortunately the last two rushes had carried the play well over to his side—the boundary was only fifteen yards away. Dink had thought out quickly
25 what he would do. He crept in closer than an end usually plays and at the snap of the ball rushed straight into the starting interference before it could gather dangerous momentum. The back, seeing him thus drawn in, instinctively swerved wide around his interference, forced
30 slightly back. Before he could turn forward his own speed and the necessity of distancing Stover and Condit drove him out of bounds for a four-yard loss.

"Second down, nine yards to go!" came the verdict.

"Rather risky going in like that," said Flash Condit,
35 who backed up his side.

"Wanted to force him out of bounds," said Stover.

"Oh—look out for something between tackle and guard now."

"No—they'll try the other side now to get a clean
5 sweep at me," said Stover.

The red-haired halfback disappeared in the opposite side and, well protected, kept his feet for five yards.

"Third down, four to gain."

"Now for a kick," said Stover, as the Andover end
10 came out opposite him. "What the deuce am I going to do to this coot to mix him up? He looks more as though he'd like to tackle me than to get past." He looked over and caught a glance from the Andover quarter. "I wonder. Why not a fake kick? They've sized me up for
15 green. I'll play it carefully."

At the play, instead of blocking, he jumped back and to one side, escaping the end, who dove at his knees. Then, rushing ahead, he stalled off the half and caught the fullback with a tackle that brought him to his feet
20 rubbing his side.

"Lawrenceville's ball. Time up for the first half."

Dink had not thought of the time. Amazed, he scrambled to his feet, half angry at the interruption, and following the team went over to the room to be talked
25 to by the captain and the coach.

It was a hang-dog crowd that gathered there, quailing under the scornful lashing of Garry Cockrell. He spared no one, he omitted no names. Dink, listening, lowered his eyes, ashamed to look upon the face of the team. One
30 or two cried out:

"Oh, I say, Garry!"

"That's too much!"

"Too much, too much, is it?" cried their captain, walking up and down, striking the flat of his hand with
35 the clenched fist. "By heavens, it's nothing to what they

are saying of us out there. They're ashamed of us, one
and all! Listen to the cheering if you don't believe it!
They'll cheer a losing team, a team that is being driven
back foot by foot. There's something glorious in that,
5 but a team that stands up to be pushed over, a team that
lies down and quits, a team that hasn't one bit of red
fighting blood in it, they won't cheer; they're ashamed of
you! Now, I'll tell you what's going to happen to you.
You're going to be run down the field for just about four
10 touchdowns. Here's Lentz being tossed around by a
fellow that weighs forty pounds less. Why, he's the joke
of the game. McCarty hasn't stopped a play, not one!
Waladoo's so easy that they rest up walking through him.
But that's not the worst, you're playing wide apart as
15 though there wasn't a man within ten miles of you; not
one of you is helping out the other. The only time you've
taken the ball from them is when a little shaver comes in
and uses his head. Now, you're not going to win this
game, but by the Almighty you're going out there and
20 going to hold that Andover team! You've got the wind
against you; you've got everything against you; you've
got to fight on your own goal line, not once but twenty
times. But you've got to hold 'em; you're going to make
good; you're going to wipe out that disgraceful, cowardly
25 first half! You're going out there to stand those fellows
off! You're going to make the school cheer for you again
as though they believed in you, as though they were
proud of you! You're going to do a bigger thing than
beat a weaker team! You're going to fight off defeat and
30 show that, if you can't win, you can't be beaten!"

Mr. Ware, in a professional way, passed from one to
another with a word of advice: "Play lower, get the jump
—don't be drawn in by a fake plunge—watch Goodhue."

But Dink heard nothing; he sat in his corner, clasping
35 and unclasping his hands, suffering with the moments

that separated him from the fray. Then all at once he
was back on the field, catching the force of the wind that
blew the hair about his temples, hearing the half-hearted
welcome that went up from the school.

5   "Hear that cheer!" said Garry Cockrell bitterly.

From Butcher Stevens' boot the ball went twisting
and veering down the field. Stover went down, dodging
instinctively, hardly knowing what he did. Then as he
started to spring at the runner an interferer from behind
10 flung himself on him and sent him sprawling, but not
until one arm had caught and checked his man.

McCarty had stopped the runner, when Dink sprang
to his feet, wild with the rage of having missed his
tackle.

15   "Steady!" cried the voice of his captain.

He lined up hurriedly, seeing red. The interference
started for him, he flung himself at it blindly and was
buried under the body of the red-haired half. Powerless
to move, humiliatingly held under the sturdy body, the
20 passion of fighting rose in him again. He tried to throw
him off, doubling up his fist, waiting until his arm was
free.

"Why, you're easy, kid," said a mocking voice. "We'll
come again."

25   The taunt suddenly chilled him. Without knowing
how it happened, he laughed.

"That's the last time you get me, old rooster," he
said, in a voice that did not belong to him.

He glanced back. Andover had gained fifteen yards.

30   "That comes from losing my head," he said quietly.
"That's over."

It had come, the cold consciousness of which Cockrell
had spoken, strange as the second wind that surprises the
distressed runner.

35   "I've got to teach that red-haired coot a lesson," he

said. "He's a little too confident. I'll shake him up a bit."

The opportunity came on the third play, with another attack on his end. He ran forward a few steps and stood 5 still, leaning a little forward, waiting for the red-haired back who came plunging at him. Suddenly Dink dropped to his knees, the interferer went violently over his back, something struck Stover in the shoulder and his arms closed with the fierce thrill of holding his man.

10 "Second down, seven yards to gain," came the welcome sound.

Time was taken out for the red-haired halfback, who had had the wind knocked out of him.

"Now he'll be more respectful," said Dink, and as 15 soon as he caught his eye he grinned. "Red hair—I'll see if I can't get his temper."

Thus checked, and to use the advantage of the wind, Andover elected to kick. The ball went twisting, and, changing its course in the strengthening wind, escaped 20 the clutches of Macnooder and went bounding toward the goal where Charlie De Soto saved it on the twenty-five-yard line. In an instant the overwhelming disparity of the sides was apparent.

A return kick at best could gain but twenty-five or 25 thirty yards. From now on they would be on the defensive.

Dink came in to support his traditional enemy, Tough McCarty. The quick, nervous voice of Charlie De Soto rose in a shriek: "Now, Lawrenceville, get into this, 30 7-52-3."

Dink swept around for a smash on the opposite tackle, head down, eyes fastened on the back before him, feeling the shock of resistance and the yielding response as he thrust forward, pushing, heaving on, until everything 35 piled up before him. Four yards gained.

A second time they repeated the play, making the first down.

"Time to spring a quick one through us," he thought.

But again De Soto elected the same play.

5   "What's he trying to do?" said Dink. "Why don't he vary it?"

Someone hauled him out of the tangled pile. It was Tough McCarty.

"Say, our tackle's a stiff one," he said, with his mouth
10 to Stover's ear. "You take his knees; I'll take him above this time."

Their signal came at last. Dink dove, trying to meet the shifting knees and throw him off his balance. The next moment a powerful arm caught him as he left the
15 ground and swept him aside.

"Any gain?" he asked anxiously as he came up.

"Only a yard," said McCarty. "He got through and smeered the play."

"I know how to get him next time," said Dink.
20   The play was repeated. This time Stover made a feint and then dove successfully after the big arm had swept fruitlessly past. Flash Condit, darting through the line, was tackled by Goodhue and fell forward for a gain.

25   "How much?" said Stover, rising joyfully.

"They're measuring."

The distance was tried and found to be two feet short of the necessary five yards. The risk was too great, a kick was signaled and the ball was Andover's, just inside
30 the center of the field.

"Now, Lawrenceville," cried the captain, "show what you're made of."

The test came quickly, a plunge between McCarty and Lentz yielded three yards, a second four. The Andover
35 attack, with the same precision as before, struck any-

where between the tackles and found holes. Dink, at the
bottom of almost every pile, raged at Tough McCarty.

"He's doing nothing, he isn't fighting," he said angrily. "He doesn't know what it is to fight. Why
5 doesn't he break up that interference for me?"

When the attack struck his end now it turned in, slic-
ing off tackle, the runner well screened by close interference that held him up when Stover tackled, dragging him
on for precious yards. Three and four yards at a time,
10 the blue advance rolled its way irresistibly toward the
red and black goal. They were inside the twenty-yard
line now.

Cockrell was pleading with them. Little Charlie De
Soto was running along the line, slapping their backs,
15 calling frantically on them to throw the blue back.

And gradually the line did stiffen, slowly but per-
ceptibly the advance was cut down. Enmities were forgotten with the shadow of the goal posts looming at their
backs. Waladoo and Turkey Reiter were fighting side
20 by side, calling to each other. Tough McCarty was haul-
ing Stover out of desperate scrimmages, patting him on
the back and calling him "good old Dink." The fighting
blood that Garry Cockrell had called upon was at last
there—the line had closed and fought together.

25 And yet they were borne back to their fifteen-yard
line, two yards at a time, just losing the fourth down.

Stover at end was trembling like a blooded terrier, on
edge for each play, shrieking:

"Oh, Tough, get through—you must get through!"

30 He was playing by intuition now, no time to plan.
He knew just who had the ball and where it was going.
Out or in, the attack was concentrating on his end—only
McCarty and he could stop it. He was getting his man,
but they were dragging him on, fighting now for inches.

35 "Third down, one yard to gain!"

"Watch my end," he shouted to Flash Condit, and hurling himself forward at the starting backs dove under the knees, and grabbing the legs about him went down buried under the mass he had upset.

5   It seemed hours before the crushing bodies were pulled off and someone's arm brought him to his feet and someone hugged him, shouting in his ear:

"You saved it, Dink, you saved it!"

Someone rushed up with a sponge and began dabbing 10 his face.

"What the deuce are they doing that for?" he said angrily.

Then he noticed that an arm was under his and he turned curiously to the face near him. It was Tough 15 McCarty's.

"Whose ball is it?" he said.

"Ours."

He looked to the other side. Garry Cockrell was supporting him.

20   "What's the matter?" he said, trying to draw his head away from the sponge that was dripping water down his throat.

"Just a little wind knocked out, youngster—coming to?"

25   "I'm all right."

He walked a few steps alone and then took his place. Things were in a daze on the horizon, but not there in the field. Everything else was shut out except his duty there.

30   Charlie De Soto's voice rose shrill:

"Now, Lawrenceville, up the field with it. This team's just begun to play. We've got together, boys. Let her rip!"

No longer scattered, but a unit, all differences forgot, 35 fighting for the same idea, the team rose up and crashed

through the Andover line, every man in the play, ten—
fifteen yards ahead.

"Again!" came the strident cry.

Without a pause the line sprang into place, formed and
5 swept forward. It was a privilege to be in such a game,
to feel the common frenzy, the awakened glance of battle
that showed down the line. Dink, side by side with
Tough McCarty, thrilled with the same thrill, plunging
ahead with the same motion, fighting the same fight; no
10 longer alone and desperate, but nerved with the consciousness of a partner whose gameness matched his own.

For thirty yards they carried the ball down the field,
before the stronger Andover team, thrown off its feet by
the unexpected frenzy, could rally and stand them off.
15 Then an exchange of punts once more drove them back
to their twenty-five-yard line.

A second time the Andover advance set out from the
fifty-yard line and slowly fought its way to surrender the
ball in the shadow of the goal posts.

20   Stover played on in a daze, remembering nothing of
the confused shock of bodies that had gone before, wondering how much longer he could hold out—to last out
the game as the captain had told him. He was groggy,
from time to time he felt the sponge's cold touch on his
25 face or heard the voice of Tough McCarty in his ear.

"Good old Dink, die game!"

How he loved McCarty fighting there by his side,
whispering to him:

"You and I, Dink! What if he is an old elephant,
30 we'll put him out of the play."

Still, flesh and blood could not last forever. The half
must be nearly up.

"Two minutes more time."

"What was that?" he said groggily to Flash Condit.
35   "Two minutes more. Hold 'em now!"

It was Andover's ball. He glanced around. They were down near the twenty-five-yard line somewhere. He looked at McCarty, whose frantic head showed against the sky.

5   "Break it up, Tough," he said, and struggled toward him.

A cry went up, the play was halted.

"He's groggy," he heard voices say, and then came the welcome splash of the sponge.

10   Slowly his vision cleared to the anxious faces around him.

"Can you last?" said the captain.

"I'm all right," he said gruffly.

"Things cleared up now?"

15   "Fine!"

McCarty put his arm about him and walked with him.

"Oh, Dink, you will last, won't you?"

"You bet I will, Tough!"

20   "It's the last stand, old boy!"

"The last."

"Only two minutes more we've got to hold 'em! The last ditch, Dink."

"I'll last."

25   He looked up and saw the school crouching along the line—tense, drawn faces. For the first time he realized they were there, calling on him to stand steadfast.

He went back, meeting the rush that came his way, half-knocked aside, half-getting his man, dragged again 30 until assistance came. De Soto's stinging hand slapped his back and the sting was good, clearing his brain.

Things came into clear outline once more. He saw down the line and to the end where Garry Cockrell stood.

"Good old captain," he said. "They'll not get by 35 me, not now."

He was in every play it seemed to him, wondering why Andover was always keeping the ball, always coming at his end. Suddenly he had a shock. Over his shoulder were the goal posts, the line he stood on was the line of
5 his own goal.

He gave a hoarse cry and went forward like a madman, parting the interference. Someone else was through; Tough was through; the whole line was through flinging back the runner. He went down
10 clinging to Goodhue, buried under a mass of his own tacklers. Then, through the frenzy, he heard the shrill call of time.

He struggled to his feet. The ball lay scarcely four yards from the glorious goal posts. Then, before the
15 school could sweep them up, panting, exhausted, they gathered in a circle with incredulous, delirious faces, and leaning heavily, wearily on one another gave the cheer for Andover. And the touch of Stover's arm on McCarty's shoulder was like an embrace.

NOTES AND SUGGESTIONS

We have been given here a very realistic picture of a modern football game. In writing a description of this kind, it is necessary for the author to do so from some definite point of view. When the point of view is established, the writer must be careful not to violate it, i.e., he must be on the lookout to tell only those things which could be seen from the standpoint chosen. It is possible for the author to change his viewpoint during the course of a description but when he does so, the reader must be made aware of that fact at once. In order to have a description clear and convincing, the reader must never be left in doubt as to the writer's point of view.

If you have read the rest of "Ivanhoe," as suggested previously, you may have noticed another description of this type, namely the account given of the storming of the Norman castle. In that passage, Rebecca describes the events as she sees them from the castle-window; she tells what is taking place to Ivanhoe who lies wounded and helpless on a couch near by.

1. Through whose eyes does the author make us see this game?
2. a. Why is this a good way to describe the game?
   b. Does the writer disregard his point of view in any part of the account?
3. a. In this description, where does the author change his point of view?
   b. What advantage is gained by the change?
4. a. Why is Dink Stover in such a nervous condition?

b. How does the author bring this out?
c. Show definitely where those places are.
5. a. What is the writer's opinion of the value of the game of football as a part of a boy's training?
   b. What qualities will the game develop according to this account?
   c. Point out specifically where the author is really presenting arguments in favor of this game.

Explanatory Notes

Page 125, line 2—"Andover"—a town in Massachusetts, near Boston; the seat of Phillips' Academy, one of the best known preparatory schools in the country.

Page 130, line 2—"Lawrenceville"—a town in New Jersey, near Princeton; the seat of the Lawrenceville Academy, another of the important preparatory schools of this country.

Suggestions for Home Reading

Johnson's "The Prodigious Hickey"—a collection of short stories of the life at Lawrenceville, by the author of the preceding selection.

Hughes' "Tom Brown's Schooldays," a story of English school life.
Kipling's "Stalky and Co.," a story of school life.

WEE WILLIE WINKIE

("An officer and a gentleman")

BY RUDYARD KIPLING

RUDYARD KIPLING is one of the great figures in the literary world of to-day. He was born in India in 1865 and was educated in England. He began his literary career as a journalist in India. He is a novelist, a short story writer, and a poet.

Wee Willie Winkie was published in 1888 in a volume of short stories. As in many other of his tales, Kipling has used the army life in India as a setting for his narrative. This selection is well worth study because of the masterly way in which it has been constructed.

His full name was Percival William Williams, but he picked up the other name in a nursery book, and that was the end of the christened titles. His mother's *ayah* called him Willie-*Baba*, but as he never paid the faintest
5 attention to anything that the *ayah* said, her wisdom did not help matters.

His father was the Colonel of the 195th, and as soon as Wee Willie Winkie was old enough to understand what Military Discipline meant, Colonel Williams put him
10 under it. There was no other way of managing the child. When he was good for a week, he drew good-conduct pay; and when he was bad, he was deprived of his good-conduct stripe. Generally he was bad, for India offers so many chances to little six-year-olds of going wrong.

15 Children resent familiarity from strangers, and Wee Willie Winkie was a very particular child. Once he accepted an acquaintance, he was graciously pleased to thaw. He accepted Brandis, a subaltern of the 195th, on sight. Brandis was having tea at the Colonel's, and Wee Willie
20 Winkie entered strong in the possession of a good-conduct badge won for not chasing the hens round the compound. He regarded Brandis with gravity for at least ten minutes, and then delivered himself of his opinion.

"I like you," said he slowly, getting off his chair and
25 coming over to Brandis. "I like you. I shall call you Coppy, because of your hair. Do you *mind* being called Coppy? It is because of ve hair, you know."

Here was one of the most embarrassing of Wee Willie Winkie's peculiarities. He would look at a stranger for
30 some time, and then, without warning or explanation,

would give him a name. And the name stuck. No regimental penalties could break Wee Willie Winkie of this habit. He lost his good-conduct badge for christening the Commissioner's wife "Pobs"; but nothing that the
5 Colonel could do made the Station forego the nickname, and Mrs. Collen remained Mrs. "Pobs" till the end of her stay. So Brandis was christened "Coppy," and rose, therefore, in the estimation of the regiment.

If Wee Willie Winkie took an interest in any one, the
10 fortunate man was envied alike by the mess and the rank and file. And in their envy lay no suspicion of self-interest. "The Colonel's son" was idolized on his own merits entirely. Yet Wee Willie Winkie was not lovely. His face was permanently freckled, as his legs were per-
15 manently scratched, and in spite of his mother's almost tearful remonstrances he had insisted upon having his long, yellow locks cut short in the military fashion. "I want my hair like Sergeant Tummil's," said Wee Willie Winkie, and his father abetting, the sacrifice was ac-
20 complished.

Three weeks after the bestowal of his youthful affections on Lieutenant Brandis—henceforth to be called "Coppy" for the sake of brevity—Wee Willie Winkie was destined to behold strange things and far beyond his
25 comprehension.

Coppy returned his liking with interest. Coppy had let him wear for five rapturous minutes his own big sword —just as tall as Wee Willie Winkie. Coppy had promised him a terrier puppy; and Coppy had permitted him
30 to witness the miraculous operation of shaving. Nay, more—Coppy had said that even he, Wee Willie Winkie, would rise in time to the ownership of a box of shiny knives, a silver soap-box and a silver-handled "sputter-brush," as Wee Willie Winkie called it. Decidedly, there
35 was no one except his father, who could give or take away

good-conduct badges at pleasure, half so wise, strong, and valiant as Coppy with the Afghan and Egyptian medals on his breast. Why, then, should Coppy be guilty of the unmanly weakness of kissing—vehemently kissing—a

5 "big girl," Miss Allardyce to wit? In the course of a morning ride, Wee Willie Winkie had seen Coppy so doing, and, like the gentleman he was, had promptly wheeled round and cantered back to his groom, lest the groom should also see.

10 Under ordinary circumstances he would have spoken to his father, but he felt instinctively that this was a matter on which Coppy ought first to be consulted.

"Coppy," shouted Wee Willie Winkie, reining up outside that subaltern's bungalow early one morning—"I

15 want to see you, Coppy!"

"Come in, young 'un," returned Coppy, who was at early breakfast in the midst of his dogs. "What mischief have you been getting into now?"

Wee Willie Winkie had done nothing notoriously bad

20 for three days, and so stood on a pinnacle of virtue.

"I've been doing nothing bad," said he, curling himself into a long chair with a studious affectation of the Colonel's languor after a hot parade. He buried his freckled nose in a teacup and, with eyes staring roundly

25 over the rim, asked:—"I say, Coppy, is it pwoper to kiss big girls?"

"By Jove! You're beginning early. Who do you want to kiss?"

"No one. My muvver's always kissing me if I don't

30 stop her. If it isn't pwoper, how was you kissing Major Allardyce's big girl last morning, by ve canal?"

Coppy's brow wrinkled. He and Miss Allardyce had with great craft managed to keep their engagement secret for a fortnight. There were urgent and imperative rea-

35 sons why Major Allardyce should not know how matters

stood for at least another month, and this small marplot had discovered a great deal too much.

"I saw you," said Wee Willie Winkie calmly. "But ve groom didn't see. I said, '*Hut jao.*'"

5 "Oh, you had that much sense, you young Rip," groaned poor Coppy, half amused and half angry. "And how many people may you have told about it?"

"Only me myself. You didn't tell when I twied to wide ve buffalo ven my pony was lame; and I fought you 10 wouldn't like."

"Winkie," said Coppy enthusiastically, shaking the small hand, "you're the best of good fellows. Look here, you can't understand all these things. One of these days —hang it, how can I make you see it!—I'm going to 15 marry Miss Allardyce, and then she'll be Mrs. Coppy, as you say. If your young mind is so scandalized at the idea of kissing big girls, go and tell your father."

"What will happen?" said Wee Willie Winkie, who firmly believed that his father was omnipotent.

20 "I shall get into trouble," said Coppy, playing his trump card with an appealing look at the holder of the ace.

"Ven I won't," said Wee Willie Winkie briefly. "But my faver says it's un-man-ly to be always kissing, and I 25 didn't fink *you'd* do vat, Coppy."

"I'm not always kissing, old chap. It's only now and then, and when you're bigger you'll do it too. Your father meant it's not good for little boys."

"Ah!" said Wee Willie Winkie, now fully enlightened. 30 "It's like ve sputter-brush?"

"Exactly," said Coppy gravely.

"But I don't fink I'll ever want to kiss big girls, nor no one, 'cept my muvver. And I *must* vat, you know."

There was a long pause, broken by Wee Willie Winkie. 35 "Are you fond of vis big girl, Coppy?"

"Awfully!" said Coppy.

"Fonder van you are of Bell or ve Butcha—or me?"

"It's in a different way," said Coppy. "You see, one
of these days Miss Allardyce will belong to me, but you'll
5 grow up and command the Regiment and—all sorts of
things. It's quite different, you see."

"Very well," said Wee Willie Winkie, rising. "If
you're fond of ve big girl, I won't tell any one. I must
go now."

10 Coppy rose and escorted his small guest to the door,
adding:—"You're the best of little fellows, Winkie. I
tell you what. In thirty days from now you can tell if
you like—tell any one you like."

Thus the secret of the Brandis-Allardyce engagement
15 was dependent on a little child's word. Coppy, who
knew Wee Willie Winkie's idea of truth, was at ease, for
he felt that he would not break promises. Wee Willie
Winkie betrayed a special and unusual interest in Miss
Allardyce, and, slowly revolving round that embarrassed
20 young lady, was used to regard her gravely with unwink-
ing eye. He was trying to discover why Coppy should
have kissed her. She was not half so nice as his own
mother. On the other hand, she was Coppy's property,
and would in time belong to him. Therefore it behooved
25 him to treat her with as much respect as Coppy's big
sword or shiny pistol.

The idea that he shared a great secret in common with
Coppy kept Wee Willie Winkie unusually virtuous for
three weeks. Then the Old Adam broke out, and he
30 made what he called a "camp fire" at the bottom of the
garden. How could he have foreseen that the flying
sparks would have lighted the Colonel's little hayrick and
consumed a week's store for the horses? Sudden and
swift was the punishment—deprivation of the good-con-
35 duct badge and, most sorrowful of all, two days confine-

ment to barracks—the house and veranda—coupled with
the withdrawal of the light of his father's countenance.

He took the sentence like the man he strove to be,
drew himself up with a quivering under-lip, saluted, and,
5 once clear of the room, ran to weep bitterly in his nursery
—called by him "my quarters." Coppy came in the
afternoon and attempted to console the culprit.

"I'm under awwest," said Wee Willie Winkie mourn-
fully, "and I didn't ought to speak to you."
10   Very early the next morning he climbed on to the roof
of the house—that was not forbidden—and beheld Miss
Allardyce going for a ride.

"Where are you going?" cried Wee Willie Winkie.

"Across the river," she answered, and trotted forward.
15   Now the cantonment in which the 195th lay was
bounded on the north by a river—dry in the winter.
From his earliest years, Wee Willie Winkie had been forbidden to go across the river, and had noted that even
Coppy—the almost almighty Coppy—had never set foot
20 beyond it. Wee Willie Winkie had once been read to, out
of a big blue book, the history of the Princess and the Goblins—a most wonderful tale of a land where the Goblins
were always warring with the children of men until they
were defeated by one Curdie. Ever since that date it
25 seemed to him that the bare black and purple hills across
the river were inhabited by Goblins, and, in truth, every
one had said that there lived the Bad Men.   Even in his
own house the lower halves of the windows were covered
with green paper on account of the Bad Men who might,
30 if allowed clear view, fire into peaceful drawing-rooms and
comfortable bedrooms. Certainly, beyond the river,
which was the end of all the Earth, lived the Bad Men.
And here was Major Allardyce's big girl, Coppy's property, preparing to venture into their borders! What would
35 Coppy say if anything happened to her?   If the Goblins

ran off with her as they did with Curdie's Princess? She
must at all hazards be turned back.

The house was still. Wee Willie Winkie reflected for
a moment on the very terrible wrath of his father; and
5 then—broke his arrest! It was a crime unspeakable. The
low sun threw his shadow, very large and very black, on
the trim garden paths, as he went down to the stables and
ordered his pony. It seemed to him in the hush of the
dawn that all the big world had been bidden to stand still
10 and look at Wee Willie Winkie guilty of mutiny. The
drowsy groom handed him his mount, and, since the one
great sin made all others insignificant, Wee Willie Winkie
said that he was going to ride over to Coppy Sahib, and
went out at a footpace, stepping on the soft mould of the
15 flower borders.

The devastating tract of the pony's feet was the last
misdeed that cut him off from all sympathy of Humanity.
He turned into the road, leaned forward, and rode as fast
as the pony could put foot to the ground in the direction
20 of the river.

But the liveliest of twelve-two ponies can do little
against the long canter of a Waler. Miss Allardyce was
far ahead, had passed through the crops, beyond the Police
post, where all the guards were asleep, and her mount
25 was scattering the pebbles of the river bed as Wee Willie
Winkie left the cantonment and British India behind him.
Bowed forward and still flogging, Wee Willie Winkie shot
into Afghan territory, and could just see Miss Allardyce
a black speck, flickering across the stony plain. The
30 reason of her wandering was simple enough. Coppy, in
a tone of too-hastily-assumed authority, had told her over
night that she must not ride out by the river. And she
had gone to prove her own spirit and teach Coppy a lesson.

Almost at the foot of the inhospitable hills, Wee Willie
35 Winkie saw the Waler blunder and come down heavily.

Miss Allardyce struggled clear, but her ankle had been
severely twisted, and she could not stand. Having thus
demonstrated her spirit, she wept copiously, and was surprised by the apparition of a white, wide-eyed child in
5 khaki, on a nearly spent pony.

"Are you badly, badly hurted?" shouted Wee Willie
Winkie, as soon as he was within range. "You didn't
ought to be here."

"I don't know," said Miss Allardyce ruefully, ignoring
10 the reproof. "Good gracious, child, what are *you* doing
here?"

"You said you was going acwoss ve wiver," panted
Wee Willie Winkie, throwing himself off his pony. "And
nobody—not even Coppy—must go acwoss ve wiver, and I
15 came after you ever so hard, but you wouldn't stop, and
now you've hurted yourself, and Coppy will be angwy wiv
me, and—I've bwoken my awwest! I've bwoken my
awwest!"

The future Colonel of the 195th sat down and sobbed.
20 In spite of the pain in her ankle the girl was moved.

"Have you ridden all the way from cantonments,
little man? What for?"

"You belonged to Coppy. Coppy told me so!"
wailed Wee Willie Winkie disconsolately. "I saw him
25 kissing you, and he said he was fonder of you van Bell
or ve Butcha or me. And so I came. You must get up
and come back. You didn't ought to be here. Vis is a
bad place, and I've bwoken my awwest."

"I can't move, Winkie," said Miss Allardyce, with a
30 groan. "I've hurt my foot. What shall I do?"

She showed a readiness to weep afresh, which steadied
Wee Willie Winkie, who had been brought up to believe
that tears were the depth of unmanliness. Still, when
one is as great a sinner as Wee Willie Winkie, even a man
35 may be permitted to break down.

"Winkie," said Miss Allardyce, "when you've rested a little, ride back and tell them to send out something to carry me back in. It hurts fearfully."

The child sat still for a little time and Miss Allardyce
5 closed her eyes; the pain was nearly making her faint. She was roused by Wee Willie Winkie tying up the reins on his pony's neck and setting it free with a vicious cut of his whip that made it whicker. The little animal headed toward the cantonments.
10 "Oh, Winkie! What are you doing?"

"Hush!" said Wee Willie Winkie. "Vere's a man coming—one of ve Bad Men. I must stay wiv you. My faver says a man must *always* look after a girl. Jack will go home, and ven vey'll come and look for us. Vat's
15 why I let him go."

Not one man but two or three had appeared from behind the rocks of the hills, and the heart of Wee Willie Winkie sank within him, for just in this manner were the Goblins wont to steal out and vex Curdie's soul. Thus
20 had they played in Curdie's garden; he had seen the picture, and thus had they frightened the Princess's nurse. He heard them talking to each other, and recognized with joy the bastard Pushto that he had picked up from one of his father's grooms lately dismissed. People who
25 spoke that tongue could not be the Bad Men. They were only natives after all.

They came up to the bowlders on which Miss Allardyce's horse had blundered.

Then rose from the rock Wee Willie Winkie, child of
30 the Dominant Race, aged six and three quarters, and said briefly and emphatically, "*Joa!*" The pony had crossed the river bed.

The men laughed, and laughter from natives was the one thing Wee Willie Winkie could not tolerate. He
35 asked them what they wanted and why they did not

154 *Readings in Literature*

depart. Other men with most evil faces and crooked-stocked guns crept out of the shadows of the hills, till soon Wee Willie Winkie was face to face with an audience some twenty strong. Miss Allardyce screamed.

5 "Who are you?" said one of the men.

"I am the Colonel Sahib's son, and my order is that you go at once. You black men are frightening the Miss Sahib. One of you must run into cantonments and take the news that the Miss Sahib has hurt herself, and that 10 the Colonel's son is here with her."

"Put our feet into the trap?" was the laughing reply. "Hear this boy's speech!"

"Say that I sent you—I, the Colonel's son. They will give you money."

15 "What is the use of this talk? Take up the child and the girl, and we can at least ask for the ransom. Ours are the villages on the heights," said a voice in the background.

These *were* the Bad Men—worse than Goblins—and 20 it needed all Wee Willie Winkie's training to prevent him from bursting into tears. But he felt that to cry before a native, excepting only his mother's *ayah*, would be an infamy greater than any mutiny. Moreover, he, as future Colonel of the 195th, had that grim regiment at his back.

25 "Are you going to carry us away?" said Wee Willie Winkie, very blanched and uncomfortable.

"Yes, my little *Sahib Bahadur*," said the tallest of the men, "and eat you afterwards."

"That is child's talk," said Wee Willie Winkie. "Men 30 do not eat men."

A yell of laughter interrupted him, but he went on firmly,—"And if you do carry us away, I tell you that all my regiment will come up in a day and kill you all without leaving one. Who will take my message to the 35 Colonel Sahib?"

Speech in any vernacular—and Wee Willie Winkie had a colloquial acquaintance with three—was easy to the boy who could not yet manage his "r's" and "th's" aright.

5　Another man joined the conference, crying:—"O foolish men! What this babe says is true. He is the heart's heart of those white troops. For the sake of peace let them both go, for if he be taken, the regiment will break loose and gut the valley. *Our* villages are in the valley, 10 and we shall not escape. That regiment are devils. They broke Khoda Yar's breastbone with kicks when he tried to take the rifles; and if we touch this child they will fire and rape and plunder for a month, till nothing remains. Better to send a man back to take the message 15 and get a reward. I say that this child is their God, and that they will spare none of us, nor our women, if we harm him."

It was Din Mahommed, the dismissed groom of the Colonel, who made the diversion, and an angry and heated 20 discussion followed. Wee Willie Winkie, standing over Miss Allardyce, waited the upshot. Surely his "wegiment," his own "wegiment," would not desert him if they knew of his extremity.

.　　.　　.　　.　　.　　.　　.　　.　　.

The riderless pony brought the news to the 195th, 25 though there had been consternation in the Colonel's household for an hour before. The little beast came in through the parade-ground in front of the main barracks where the men were settling down to play Spoil-five till the afternoon. Devlin, the Color Sergeant of E Com-30 pany, glanced at the empty saddle and tumbled through the barrack-rooms, kicking up each Room Corporal as he passed. "Up, ye beggars! There's something happened to the Colonel's son," he shouted.

"He couldn't fall off! S'elp me, 'e *couldn't* fall off,"
blubbered a drummer boy. "Go an' hunt acrost the
river. He's over there if he's anywhere, an' maybe
those Pathans have got 'im. For the love o' Gawd
5 don't look for 'im in the nullahs! Let's go over the
river."

"There's sense in Mott yet," said Devlin. "E Company, double out to the river—sharp!"

So E Company, in its shirt sleeves mainly, doubled for
10 the dear life, and in the rear toiled the perspiring Sergeant, adjuring it to double yet faster. The cantonment
was alive with the men of the 195th hunting for Wee Willie
Winkie, and the Colonel finally overtook E Company, far
too exhausted to swear, struggling in the pebbles of the
15 river bed.

Up the hill under which Wee Willie Winkie's Bad Men
were discussing the wisdom of carrying off the child and
the girl, a lookout fired two shots.

"What have I said?" shouted Din Mahommed.
20 "There is the warning! The *pulton* are out already and
are coming across the plain! Get away! Let us not be
seen with the boy!"

The men waited for an instant, and then, as another
shot was fired, withdrew into the hills, silently as they had
25 appeared.

"The wegiment is coming," said Wee Willie Winkie
confidently to Miss Allardyce, "and it's all wight. Don't
cwy!"

He needed the advice himself, for ten minutes later,
30 when his father came up, he was weeping bitterly with
his head in Miss Allardyce's lap.

And the men of the 195th carried him home with
shouts and rejoicings; and Coppy, who had ridden a horse
into a lather, met him, and, to his intense disgust, kissed
35 him openly in the presence of the men.

But there was balm for his dignity. His father assured him that not only would the breaking of arrest be condoned, but that the good-conduct badge would be restored as soon as his mother could sew it on his blouse 5 sleeve. Miss Allardyce had told the Colonel a story that made him proud of his son.

"She belonged to you, Coppy," said Wee Willie Winkie, indicating Miss Allardyce with a grimy forefinger. "I *knew* she didn't ought to go acwoss ve wiver, 10 and I knew ve wegiment would come to me if I sent Jack home."

"You're a hero, Winkie," said Coppy—"a *pukka* hero!"

"I don't know what vat means," said Wee Willie 15 Winkie, "but you mustn't call me Winkie any no more. I'm Percival Will'am Will'ams."

And in this manner did Wee Willie Winkie enter into his manhood.

NOTES AND SUGGESTIONS

The title of a story is frequently a very important factor in the success or failure of the piece. There are certain rules or principles governing this phase of the work. They may be summarized briefly as follows: first, a title must not be misleading, i.e., it must give us some idea of what the story is going to be about; second, it must be interesting, i.e., it must be phrased in such a manner that it will be apt to attract readers; third, it must be short. Brevity is apt to add to the vividness of the impression made.

1. a. Using the above standards, comment on the title of this story.
   b. Point out how the theme is suggested by the title and subtitle.
   c. What is the theme of this story?

This story is splendidly constructed. A study of its structure will help to make you realize that great care is required in the arrangement of the material in order to gain a desired effect. In analyzing the story, we might make an outline as follows:

PART I.

"WEE WILLIE WINKIE"

Paragraphs
1   His name.
2   His bringing up (Military discipline).
3, 4, 5 Childish traits. Beginning of "Winkie's" regard for "Coppy."
6   The soldiers' love for "Winkie." Winkie's appearance.
7   A connecting paragraph.

PART II.

"WINKIE" AND "COPPY"

8   Mutual affection of Winkie and Coppy. Miss A—— and the incident of the kissing. Dialogue between Winkie and Coppy.
9 to 36 Concerning what Winkie had seen. Winkie entrusted with the secret of Coppy's engagement to Miss A——.
36, 37, 38 Connecting paragraphs (*Burning of the hayrick* and Winkie's punishment.)

PART III.

"WINKIE" AND MISS A——

39, 40, 41 Winkie learns that Miss A—— is going across the river.

Paragraphs
42   Winkie's knowledge of the dangerous locality.
43, 44   Winkie breaks his arrest and follows her.
45   The ride.
46   The accident.
47 to 56 Dialogue—Why Winkie followed. Plans to get help.
56, 57, 58 Winkie sets his pony free. Reason for doing so.
59 to 73 The "Bad Men." The child's bravery. The danger.
74, 75   The "Bad Men" in doubt. Din Mohammed.

PART IV.

THE RESCUE

76 to 79 The arrival of Winkie's pony at the barracks. The effect.
80 to 89 The finding of Winkie and Miss A——.
89, 90   The child's name.

2. In reading this story a second time, see if you can find any incidents that have no bearing on the theme.
3. Note the beginning and the end of the story (1st and last paragraph). Keeping those in mind, comment on the picture which Kipling is holding up for us to view.
4. Study the portions of the story told in dialogue.

Note how the author makes his characters act as well as talk.

What effect is gained by doing that?

Suggestions for Home Reading

Thomas Nelson Page's "Nancy Pansy"—a story of the Civil War, in which a little girl of eight plays the important part. Dickens' "David Copperfield."—

In the early chapters (David's departure for school and his school life), you are shown a wonderfully pathetic picture of a lovable little boy.

INTRODUCTION TO THE POETICAL SELECTIONS

THE poems that follow have been selected in order to bring out in a definite way some of the characteristics of lyric poetry.

The first five, Shelley's "To a Skylark," Keats' "Ode to a Nightingale," Burns' "To a Daisy," Wordsworth's "The Daffodils" and Herrick's "To Daffodils," have been classed together because they are poems that are expressive of thoughts and feelings that are pure and beautiful, inspired by things of Nature. One of the essentials of poetry is that the thought expressed must be elevating and ennobling. It is natural that a poet's individuality will be shown in his writings. Therefore, it is necessary for you to seek for evidences of the personality of the author in your interpretation of his work.

The two short lyrics of Tennyson have been given in order to bring to your notice poems wherein the theme is very personal in character. Here again, however, the thought is reverential and inspiring.

Scott's two poems have been chosen in order to bring out another characteristic of poetry—namely, the rhythm. Before you study these poems it will be necessary for you to find out something about rhythm and meter. You will then be in a position to appreciate the different effects that can be gained by the use of different meters.

The two poems of Browning have been selected in order to show you that poems of this type may tell a story. It is to be noted, however, that the story presents a moral or truth that is inspiring.

Six sonnets have been printed so that you may learn something of this important literary form.

Two patriotic lyrics have been given in order to remind you that a love of country always has been and always will be a fitting theme for the poet's song.

To summarize briefly, then, it is the purpose of this book to show you by these selections that by poetry we mean the expression of beautiful thoughts in language that is rhythmic in arrangement, melodious in sound and figurative and artistic in construction.

TO A SKYLARK

BY PERCY BYSSHE SHELLEY

PERCY BYSSHE SHELLEY, who was born in England in 1792 and died in 1822, was a man who rebelled at all restraint. In matters of domestic life, of religion, of government, he was imbued with a passionate desire for freedom. He was expelled from Oxford because of a pamphlet he wrote against religion. Like most of the writers of this time, Shelley was deeply influenced by the struggle of the French people for liberty. In some of his longer poems he sets forth his ideals in regard to matters of government. In his view of life, ideal happiness can result only from absolute freedom.

It seems natural, then, that Shelley should be inspired by the song of a lark—a bird that sings joyously as it mounts high into the bright morning air. Everything about this bird is typical of unrestrained happiness.

Here are the thoughts that have been aroused in this poet by the song of a skylark.

> HAIL to thee, blithe Spirit!
>   Bird thou never wert,
> That from heaven, or near it
>   Pourest thy full heart
> 5 In profuse strains of unpremeditated art.
>
>   Higher still and higher
>   From the earth thou springest,
> Like a cloud of fire,
>   The blue deep thou wingest,
> 10 And singing still dost soar, and soaring ever singest.
>
>   In the golden lightning
>   Of the sunken sun
> O'er which clouds are brightening,
>   Thou dost float and run,
> 15 Like an unbodied joy whose race is just begun.

The pale purple even
  Melts around thy flight;
Like a star of heaven
  In the broad daylight
20 Thou art unseen, but yet I hear thy shrill delight:

  Keen as are the arrows
    Of that silver sphere,
Whose intense lamp narrows
    In the white dawn clear
25 Until we hardly see, we feel that it is there.

  All the earth and air
    With thy voice is loud,
As, when night is bare,
    From one lonely cloud
30 The moon rains out her beams, and heaven is overflow'd.

  What thou art we know not;
    What is most like thee?
From rainbow clouds there flow not
    Drops so bright to see
35 As from thy presence showers a rain of melody;—

  Like a poet hidden
    In the light of thought,
Singing hymns unbidden,
    Till the world is wrought
40 To sympathy with hopes and fears it heeded not:

  Like a high-born maiden
    In a palace tower,
Soothing her love-laden
    Soul in secret hour
45 With music sweet as love, which overflows her bower:

Like a glow-worm golden
  In a dell of dew,
Scattering unbeholden
  Its aerial hue
50 Among the flowers and grass, which screen it from the
      view:

Like a rose embower'd
  In its own green leaves,
By warm winds deflower'd,
  Till the scent it gives
55 Makes faint with too much sweet these heavy-winged
      thieves.

Sound of vernal showers
  On the twinkling grass,
Rain-awakened flowers,
  All that ever was
60 Joyous, and clear, and fresh, thy music doth surpass.

Teach us, sprite or bird,
  What sweet thoughts are thine:
I have never heard
  Praise of love or wine
65 That panted forth a flood of rapture so divine.

Chorus hymeneal
  Or triumphal chaunt
Match'd with thine, would be all
  But an empty vaunt—
70 A thing wherein we feel there is some hidden want.

What objects are the fountains
  Of thy happy strain?
What fields, or waves, or mountains?
  What shapes of sky or plain?
75 What love of thine own kind? What ignorance of pain?

With thy clear keen joyance
    Languor cannot be:
Shadow of annoyance
    Never came near thee:
80 Thou lovest; but ne'er knew love's sad satiety.

Waking or asleep
    Thou of death must deem
Things more true and deep
    Than we mortals dream,
85 Or how could thy notes flow in such a crystal stream?

We look before and after,
    And pine for what is not:
Our sincerest laughter
    With some pain is fraught;
90 Our sweetest songs are those that tell of saddest thought.

Yet if we could scorn
    Hate, and pride, and fear;
If we were things born
    Not to shed a tear,
95 I know not how thy joy we ever should come near.

Better than all measures
    Of delightful sound,
Better than all treasures
    That in books are found,
100 Thy skill to poet were, thou scorner of the ground!

Teach me half the gladness
    That thy brain must know,
Such harmonious madness
    From my lips would flow,
105 The world would listen then, as I am listening now!

NOTES AND SUGGESTIONS

1. Note carefully the construction of this poem. Stanzas 1 to 7, are in eulogy of the bird.

a. What things about the lark does Shelley praise?

b. Should the lines be read slowly or rapidly? Why?

c. Explain "unpremeditated art."

2. In stanzas 7 to 15, the poet attempts to find a suitable comparison for the joy and freedom of this bird.

Explain those similes, in your own words.

3. In stanzas 15 to 21, the poet speculates on the possible cause of the joy of the lark and contrasts the lot of the bird with that of human beings.

Explain—"We look before and after——."

What does the poet mean by the line, "Our sweetest songs are those that tell of saddest thought?"

What does that line imply?

4. Tell, in your own words, the subject matter of stanza 21.

5. Why is this stanza a fitting summary of the thoughts expressed in the poem?

ODE TO A NIGHTINGALE

BY JOHN KEATS

JOHN KEATS was born in England in 1795 and died in 1821. He lived at the same time as Shelley but was one of the few writers of that period who was unaffected by the events that were taking place about him. He was handicapped by a lack of university training and by ill health. He was a victim of lung trouble which caused his death at the age of twenty-six. The fact that he knew that he was doomed, colored his whole view of life and took away, no doubt, much of his interest in the material happenings that were taking place.

The poem that follows gives us the thoughts that were inspired in this poet by the song of a nightingale. Try to imagine him on a summer's evening in a leafy grove listening to the sad beautiful notes of this bird. Note how his own sufferings are hinted at in the

longing he expresses to be free from the "weariness, the fever and
the fret" of existence here.

My heart aches, and a drowsy numbness pains
  My sense, as though of hemlock I had drunk,
Or emptied some dull opiate to the drains
  One minute past, and Lethe-wards had sunk:
5 'Tis not through envy of thy happy lot,
  But being too happy in thy happiness,—
    That thou, light-winged Dryad of the trees,
      In some melodious plot
  Of beechen green, and shadows numberless,
10   Singest of summer in full-throated ease.

O, for a draught of vintage! that hath been
  Cool'd a long age in the deep-delved earth,
Tasting of Flora and the country green,
  Dance, and Provencal song, and sunburnt mirth!
15 O for a beaker full of the warm South,
  Full of the true, the blushful Hippocrene,
    With beaded bubbles winking at the brim,
      And purple-stained mouth;
  That I might drink, and leave the world unseen,
20   And with thee fade away into the forest dim:

Fade far away, dissolve, and quite forget
  What thou among the leaves hast never known,
The weariness, the fever, and the fret
  Here, where men sit and hear each other groan;
25 Where palsy shakes a few, sad, last gray hairs,
  Where youth grows pale, and spectre-thin, and dies;
    Where but to think is to be full of sorrow
      And leaden-eyed despairs;
  Where Beauty cannot keep her lustrous eyes,
30   Or new Love pine at them beyond to-morrow.

Away! away! for I will fly to thee,
    Not charioted by Bacchus and his pards,
But on the viewless wings of Poesy,
    Though the dull brain perplexes and retards:
35 Already with thee! tender is the night,
      And haply the Queen-Moon is on her throne,
        Cluster'd around by all her starry Fays;
          But here there is no light,
    Save what from heaven is with breezes blown
40   Through verdurous glooms and winding mossy ways.

    I cannot see what flowers are at my feet,
    Nor what soft incense hangs upon the boughs,
But, in embalmed darkness, guess each sweet
    Wherewith the seasonable month endows
45 The grass, the thicket, and the fruit-tree wild;
      White hawthorn, and the pastoral eglantine;
        Fast fading violets cover'd up in leaves;
          And mid-May's eldest child,
    The coming musk-rose, full of dewy wine,
50   The murmurous haunt of flies on summer eves.

Darkling I listen; and for many a time
    I have been half in love with easeful Death,
Call'd him soft names in many a mused rhyme,
    To take into the air my quiet breath;
55 Now more than ever seems it rich to die,
      To cease upon the midnight with no pain,
        While thou art pouring forth thy soul abroad
          In such an ecstasy!
    Still wouldst thou sing, and I have ears in vain—
60   To thy high requiem become a sod.

Thou wast not born for death, immortal Bird!
No hungry generations tread thee down;
The voice I hear this passing night was heard
In ancient days by emperor and clown:
65 Perhaps the self-same song that found a path
Through the sad heart of Ruth, when, sick for home,
She stood in tears amid the alien corn;
The same that oft-times hath
Charm'd magic casements, opening on the foam
70   Of perilous seas, in faery lands forlorn.

Forlorn! the very word is like a bell
To toll me back from thee to my sole self!
Adieu! the fancy cannot cheat so well
As she is famed to do, deceiving elf.
75 Adieu! adieu! thy plaintive anthem fades
Past the near meadows, over the still stream,
Up the hillside; and now 'tis buried deep
In the next valley-glades:
Was it a vision, or a waking dream?
80   Fled is that music:—Do I wake or sleep?

NOTES AND SUGGESTIONS

1. a. Compare the first stanza of this poem with the opening stanza of Shelley's Ode.
   b. Note the different effects gained in each case.
   c. What mechanical differences in construction account in part, at least, for the differences in tone?
2. a. Tell, in your own words, the desire Keats expresses in the second and third stanzas.
   b. How do you account for the feelings expressed in those stanzas?
3. a. What things of Nature are spoken of in the fourth and fifth stanzas?
   b. How does he speak of them?
4. In stanza six, note the same desire that we spoke of previously.
5. According to the poet's speculation in stanza seven, who else probably

listened to this same song, long ages ago?

6. a. How is the poet brought out of his reverie?

b. Note the last word of stanza 7, and the first word of stanza 8.

What does he compare that word with?

c. What contrast is again brought out in the last stanza?

7. Of whom is the poet thinking in lines 61 and 62?

Explanatory Notes

Page 166, line 4—"Lethe-wards"— In Greek mythology, Lethe was one of the streams of Hades, the water of which possessed the property of making those who drank of it forget their former existence.

Page 166, line 7—"Dryad"—In classic mythology, a wood nymph.

Page 166, line 13—"Flora"—In Roman mythology, the goddess of flowers and spring.

Page 166, line 16—"Hippocrene" —a fountain on Mount Helicon, sacred to the Muses.

Page 167, line 32—"Bacchus"—In Greek mythology, the god of wine.

Page 167, line 60—"requiem"—a Mass said or sung for a departed soul.

Page 168, line 66—"Ruth"—a Biblical character, left her home and traveled to Bethlehem to make her new home with Boaz and his people.

TO A MOUNTAIN DAISY

(On turning one down with a plough in April, 1786)

BY ROBERT BURNS

ROBERT BURNS, who was born in Scotland in 1759 and died in 1796, was the oldest child of a poor Scotch farmer. He received a very meager education. The greater part of his life was given up to a struggle against poverty. In spite of his cheerless surroundings and his discouraging fight against starvation, the poetic nature that was in the man found expression in poems and ballads that will live forever.

The following poem tells us his thoughts on destroying a wild mountain flower in the course of his ploughing.

WEE, modest, crimson-tipped flow'r,
Thou's met me in an evil hour;
For I maun crush amang the stoure
    Thy slender stem.
5   To spare thee now is past my pow'r,
      Thou bonnie gem.

Alas! it's no thy neebor sweet,
The bonnie lark, companion meet,
Bending thee 'mang the dewy weet!
10   Wi' spreckl'd breast,
When upward-springing, blythe to greet
      The purpling east.

Cauld blew the bitter-biting north
Upon thy early, humble birth;
15   Yet cheerfully thou glinted forth
      Amid the storm,
Scarce rear'd above the parent-earth
      Thy tender form.

The flaunting flow'rs our gardens yield,
20   High shelt'ring woods and wa's maun shield;
But thou, beneath the random bield
      O' clod or stane,
Adorns the histie stibble-field,
      Unseen, alane.

25   There, in thy scanty mantle clad,
Thy snawie bosom sun-ward spread,
Thou lifts thy unassuming head
      In humble guise;
But now the share uptears thy bed,
30   And low thou lies!

Such is the fate of simple Bard,
On life's rough ocean luckless starr'd!
Unskilful he to note the card
    Of prudent lore,
35   Till billows rage, and gales blow hard,
    And whelm him o'er!

Such fate to suffering Worth is giv'n,
Who long with wants and woes has striv'n,
By human pride or cunning driv'n,
40   To mis'ry's brink,
Till, wrench'd of ev'ry stay but Heav'n,
    He, ruin'd, sink!

Ev'n thou who mourn'st the Daisy's fate,
That fate is thine—no distant date;
45   Stern Ruin's ploughshare drives elate,
    Full on thy bloom,
Till crush'd beneath the furrow's weight,
    Shall be thy doom!

NOTES AND SUGGESTIONS

1. Repeat, in your own words, the thoughts expressed in each of the first five stanzas.
2. What is the general topic of that part of the poem?
3. What facts about the flower, does the poet tell us indirectly, in these stanzas?
4. What comparison does he make in stanza four?
5. Pick out expressions in this poem, that, in your opinion, indicate the poet's love for Nature as represented by the daisy.
6. Explain the figure of speech in stanza five.
7. In stanzas six and seven, what comparison does Burns make?
8. Note the sad tone in the last stanza. In it to whom does he refer?

Explanatory Notes

Page 170, line 3—"stoure" means "dust."

Page 170, line 20—"wa's maun" means "walls must."

Page 170, line 21—"bield" means "shelter."

Page 170, line 23—"histie" means "dry," "barren."

THE DAFFODILS

BY WILLIAM WORDSWORTH

WILLIAM WORDSWORTH, who was born in England in 1770 and died in 1850, had all the advantages of education and travel. He lived a long life that was comparatively free from care and worry. Wordsworth spent many years in the country and grew to love the works of nature, the fields and streams, the birds and flowers. Many of his poems show this love and reverence for the works of God.

In reading the following poem, try to picture this man, on a day in early spring while the trees are still bare and many of the signs of winter still linger, walking through a lonely countryside and coming suddenly on a field of bright beautiful flowers. Here are the thoughts inspired by such a sight:

> I WANDER'D lonely as a cloud
> That floats on high o'er vales and hills,
> When all at once I saw a crowd,
> A host of golden daffodils,
> 5   Beside the lake, beneath the trees,
> Fluttering and dancing in the breeze.
>
> Continuous as the stars that shine
> And twinkle on the milky way,
> They stretch'd in never-ending line
> 10   Along the margin of a bay:
> Ten thousand saw I at a glance
> Tossing their heads in sprightly dance.
>
> The waves beside them danced, but they
> Out-did the sparkling waves in glee:—
> 15   A Poet could not but be gay
> In such a jocund company!
> I gazed—and gazed—but little thought
> What wealth the show to me had brought;

For oft, when on my couch I lie
20   In vacant or in pensive mood
They flash upon that inward eye
Which is the bliss of solitude;
And then my heart with pleasure fills,
And dances with the daffodils.

NOTES AND SUGGESTIONS

1.   Describe, in your own words, the picture painted by the poet in the first three stanzas.

2. a. Point out the figures of speech in stanza one.
   b. Explain them.
   c. Why are they suitable?

3.   Do the same thing with stanza two, in regard to the figures of speech.

4.   What effect is produced by the reading of the first three stanzas?

5.   What "wealth" was brought to the poet by the picture he has described?

6.   What is the substance of the last stanza?

7.   In your opinion, why should the remembrance of the sight bring him happiness?

TO DAFFODILS

BY ROBERT HERRICK

ROBERT HERRICK was born in England in 1591 and died in 1674. He began his university training at Cambridge as a student of law but later gave up that study for theology. In 1629, he accepted the living at Dean Prior where the greater part of his life was spent. His work in the field of literature was casual and confined entirely to lyric poetry. His poetry is characterized by a refinement of thought and gracefulness of meter that makes it very pleasing.

FAIR Daffodils, we weep to see
You haste away so soon:
As yet the early-rising Sun
Has not attain'd his noon.

5   Stay, stay,
Until the hasting day
          Has run
But to the even-song;
And, having pray'd together, we
10   Will go with you along.

We have short time to stay, as you
We have as short a Spring;
As quick a growth to meet decay
As you or any thing.
15   We die,
As your hours do, and dry
          Away
Like to the Summer's rain;
Or as the pearls of morning's dew
20   Ne'er to be found again.

NOTES AND SUGGESTIONS

1. In lines 1 and 2, why does the poet express regret?
2. What is the implied meaning in the lines from 3 through 10?
3. Explain the figure of speech in lines 9 and 10.
4. Tell, in your own words, the substance of stanza 2.
5. Explain the similes in lines 16 through 20.
6. In what way are the figures of speech used throughout the poem suitable?

BREAK, BREAK, BREAK

BY ALFRED TENNYSON

ALFRED TENNYSON was born in England in 1809 and died in 1892. For over fifty years he was the leading figure in the English literary world. He succeeded Wordsworth as Poet Laureate. His writings are many in number and varied in character. They are all, however, characterized by grace of meter and beauty of expression. Tennyson was deeply religious and the spiritual phase of his nature is shown in many of his poems. Two of his short lyrics are given here.

The first one, "Break, Break, Break," expresses the poet's feelings in meditating on the death of a friend. The loss of a loved one has turned his thoughts to the wonder and the mystery of life and death. In reading this poem, think of the author as standing alone, looking off at the ocean; children are playing on the shore; away off on the distant horizon he sees ships moving slowly along; and all the time he is conscious of the beating of the waves on the shore.

> BREAK, break, break,
>   On thy cold gray stones, O Sea!
> And I would that my tongue could utter
>   The thoughts that arise in me.
>
> 5 O well for the fisherman's boy,
>   That he shouts with his sister at play!
> O well for the sailor lad,
>   That he sings in his boat on the bay!
>
> And the stately ships go on
> 10 To their haven under the hill;
> But O for the touch of a vanish'd hand
>   And the sound of a voice that is still!
>
> Break, break, break,
>   At the foot of thy crags, O Sea!
> 15 But the tender grace of a day that is dead
>   Will never come back to me.

NOTES AND SUGGESTIONS

1. What was the poet's mood in writing this poem?
2. Why does he speak of the children, in the second stanza?
3. What thoughts about his own life do they suggest?
4. Why should he think of that at such a time or in connection with the other thoughts that were present in his mind?
5. What is the implied meaning in his mention of "the stately ships"?
6. What is "the haven under the hill"?
7. Tell, in your own words, the

meaning of the next two lines.

8. Notice that Tennyson begins the first and the last stanzas, with the same words; he is conscious, all through his reverie, of the unceasing, relentless pounding of the waves on the rocks. What do you think he means to refer to in our lives, that might be suggested by the breaking of the waves on the shore?

CROSSING THE BAR

BY ALFRED TENNYSON

SUNSET and evening star,
　And one clear call for me!
And may there be no moaning of the bar,
　When I put out to sea,

5　But such a tide as moving seems asleep,
　Too full for sound and foam,
When that which drew from out the boundless deep
　Turns again home.

Twilight and evening bell,
10　And after that the dark!
And may there be no sadness of farewell,
　When I embark;

For tho' from out our bourne of Time and Place
　The flood may bear me far,
15 I hope to see my Pilot face to face
　When I have cross'd the bar.

NOTES AND SUGGESTIONS

1. "Sunset and evening star"—what does the poet tell us about himself by this line?
2. Explain the second line.
3. What is the voyage he is going to make?
4. Explain the implied meaning of the second stanza.

5. "Twilight and e v e n i n g bell"—h o w d o e s the thought here differ from the thought expressed in the first line?

6. "And after that the dark" —what is the implied meaning of this line?

7. a. Who is the "Pilot"?

b. What is the name of that figure of speech?

8. Show how this figure of speech is in keeping with other figures used in this poem.

9. What phase of Tennyson's nature does this poem show?

BOAT SONG

(From "The Lady of the Lake")

BY SIR WALTER SCOTT

HAIL to the Chief who in triumph advances!
Honored and blessed be the ever-green Pine!
Long may the tree, in his banner that glances,
Flourish, the shelter and grace of our line!
5   Heaven send it happy dew,
Earth lend it sap anew,
Gayly to bourgeon and broadly to grow,
While every Highland glen
Sends our shout back again,
10 "Roderigh Vich Alpine dhu, ho! ieroe!"

Ours is no sapling, chance-sown by the fountain,
Blooming at Beltane, in winter to fade;
When the whirlwind has stripped every leaf on the
mountain,
The more shall Clan-Alpine exult in her shade.
15   Moored in the rifted rock,
Proof to the tempest's shock,
Firmer he roots him the ruder it blow;
Menteith and Breadalbane, then,
Echo his praise again,
20 "Roderigh Vich Alpine dhu, ho! ieroe!"

Proudly our pibroch has thrilled in Glen Fruin,
　And Bannochar's groans to our slogan replied;
Glen Luss and Ross-dhu, they are smoking in ruin,
　And the best of Loch Lomond lie dead on her side.
25　　Widow and Saxon maid
　　Long shall lament our raid,
　Think of Clan-Alpine with fear and with woe:
　　Lennox and Leven-glen
　　Shake when they hear again,
30　"Roderigh Vich Alpine dhu, ho! ieroe!"

Row, vassals, row, for the pride of the Highlands!
　Stretch to your oars for the ever-green Pine!
O that the rosebud that graces yon islands
　Were wreathed in a garland around him to twine!
35　　O that some seedling gem,
　　Worthy such noble stem,
　Honored and blessed in their shadow might grow!
　　Loud should Clan-Alpine then
　　Ring from her deepmost glen,
40　"Roderigh Vich Alpine dhu, ho! ieroe!"

NOTES AND SUGGESTIONS

1. a. What is meant by rhythm in poetry?
   b. What is meant by meter?
   c. Explain some of the different arrangements that are possible.
2. a. Take the first line of this poem, and point out where the accented syllables come.
   b. Read the line, placing strong emphasis on each accented syllable in the line. Does this mechanical arrangement bring about a slow or rapid movement in reading the line?
   c. Do the same thing with each of the following three lines.
   d. Note the 5th and 6th lines. What effect is gained by inserting these short lines?
3. Note the preponderance of short vowel sounds in the words of this poem. What is the effect of such a usage?
4. Explain how the mechanical aspect of the work is consistent with the theme.

Explanatory Notes

Page 177, line 7—"bourgeon"— from the French, meaning, "to sprout," "to put forth buds." Page 177, line 12—"Beltane"—the first day of May. An ancient Celtic festival used to be ob- served in Scotland on that day. The places referred to in the poem are all located in and about the district of Perthshire, in Scotland.

CORONACH

(From "The Lady of the Lake")

BY SIR WALTER SCOTT

He is gone on the mountain,
  He is lost to the forest,
Like a summer-dried fountain,
  When our need was the sorest.
5   The font, re-appearing,
  From the rain-drops shall borrow,
But to us comes no cheering,
  To Duncan no morrow!

The hand of the reaper
10   Takes the ears that are hoary,
But the voice of the weeper
  Wails manhood in glory.
The autumn winds rushing
  Waft the leaves that are searest,
15   But our flower was in flushing,
  When blighting was nearest.

Fleet foot on the correi,
  Sage counsel in cumber,
Red hand in the foray,
20   How sound is thy slumber!

Like the dew on the mountain,
Like the foam on the river,
Like the bubble on the fountain,
Thou art gone, and forever!

NOTES AND SUGGESTIONS

1. a. In the first line of this poem, point out where the accented s y l l a b l e s come.
   b. How does this arrangement differ from the one used in the "Boat Song"?
   c. What difference in the use of long and short vowel sounds, do you notice?
   d. Compare the general tone of this poem with that of the preceding one.
2. What is the theme of this poem?
3. Explain the figures of speech used in the second stanza.

Explanatory Notes

"Coronach"—a Gaelic word, meaning, "a funeral song," "a dirge," poured forth by the mourners over the body of the deceased.

Page 179, line 17—"correi"—a covert on a hillside.
Page 179, line 18—"cumber"— trouble.

HOW THEY BROUGHT THE GOOD NEWS FROM GHENT TO AIX

BY ROBERT BROWNING

ROBERT BROWNING, who was born in England in 1812 and died in 1889, was a celebrated English poet. He was second only to Tennyson in the literary world of the latter half of the nineteenth century. His poetry is characterized by vigor and power of thought and expression but unfortunately much of it is very difficult to understand.

I SPRANG to the stirrup, and Joris, and he;
I gallop'd, Dirck gallop'd, we gallop'd all three;

"Good speed!" cried the watch, as the gate-bolts un-
    drew;
"Speed!" echoed the wall to us galloping through;
5 Behind shut the postern, the lights sank to rest,
And into the midnight we gallop'd abreast.

Not a word to each other; we kept the great pace
Neck by neck, stride by stride, never changing our place;
I turn'd in my saddle and made its girths tight,
10 Then shorten'd each stirrup, and set the pique right,
  Rebuckled the cheek-strap, chain'd slacker the bit,
Nor gallop'd less steadily Roland a whit.

'Twas moonset at starting; but while we drew near
Lokeren, the cocks crew and twilight dawn'd clear;
15 At Boom, a great yellow star came out to see;
At Duffield, 'twas morning as plain as could be;
And from Mechelm church-steeple we heard the half
    chime,
So Joris broke silence with, "Yet there is time!"

At Aershot, up leap'd of a sudden the sun,
20 And against him the cattle stood black every one,
To stare through the mist at us galloping past,
And I saw my stout galloper Roland at last,
With resolute shoulders, each butting away
The haze, as some bluff river headland its spray:

25 And his low head and crest, just one sharp ear bent back
For my voice, and the other prick'd out on his track;
And one eye's black intelligence,—ever that glance
O'er its white edge at me, his own master, askance!
And the thick heavy spume-flakes which aye and anon
30 His fierce lips shook upwards in galloping on.

By Hasselt, Dirck groan'd; and cried Joris, "Stay spur!
Your Roos gallop'd bravely, the fault's not in her,
We'll remember at Aix"—for one heard the quick wheeze
Of her chest, saw the stretch'd neck and staggering knees,
35 And sunk tail, and horrible heave of the flank,
As down on her haunches she shudder'd and sank.

So we were left galloping, Joris and I,
Past Looz and past Tongres, no cloud in the sky;
The broad sun above laugh'd a pitiless laugh,
40 'Neath our feet broke the brittle bright stubble like chaff;
Till over by Dalhem a dome-spire sprang white,
And "Gallop," gasped Joris, "for Aix is in sight!

"How they'll greet us!"—and all in a moment his roan
Roll'd neck and croup over, lay dead as a stone;
45 And there was my Roland to bear the whole weight
Of the news which alone could save Aix from her fate,
With his nostrils like pits full of blood to the brim,
And with circles of red for his eye-sockets' rim.

Then I cast loose my buff-coat, each holster let fall,
50 Shook off both my jack-boots, let go belt and all,
Stood up in the stirrup, lean'd, patted his ear,
Call'd my Roland his pet-name, my horse without peer;
Clapp'd my hands, laugh'd and sang, any noise, bad or
        good,
Till at length into Aix Roland gallop'd and stood.

55 And all I remember is, friends flocking round
As I sat with his head 'twixt my knees on the ground;
And no voice but was praising this Roland of mine,
As I pour'd down his throat our last measure of wine,
Which (the burgesses voted by common consent)
60 Was no more than his due who brought good news from
        Ghent.

NOTES AND SUGGESTIONS

1. a. In your own words, repeat the story told in this poem.
   b. What was the "good news"?
   c. What qualities of horse and rider are brought out in the course of the poem?
   d. Which is the more important figure, the horse or the rider?

2. a. Note the rhythm.
   b. What is the effect gained?
   c. How must the lines be read?
3. Where are the places mentioned in the poem?
4. Pick out the stanzas which emphasize the good qualities of the horse.

AN INCIDENT OF THE FRENCH CAMP

BY ROBERT BROWNING

You know, we French storm'd Ratisbon:
  A mile or so away
On a little mound, Napoleon
  Stood on our storming-day;
5 With neck out-thrust, you fancy how,
  Legs wide, arms lock'd behind,
As if to balance the prone brow
  Oppressive with its mind.

Just as perhaps he mus'd "My plans
10   That soar, to earth may fall,
Let once my army-leader Lannes
  Waver at yonder wall,"—
Out 'twixt the battery-smokes there flew
  A rider, bound on bound
15 Full-galloping; nor bridle drew
  Until he reach'd the mound.

Then off there flung in smiling joy,
  And held himself erect
By just his horse's mane, a boy:
20   You hardly could suspect—

(So tight he kept his lips compress'd,
　Scarce any blood came through)
You look'd twice ere you saw his breast
　Was all but shot in two.

25　"Well," cried he, "Emperor, by God's grace
　We've got you Ratisbon!
The Marshal's in the market-place,
　And you'll be there anon
To see your flag-bird flap his vans
30　　Where I, to heart's desire,
Perch'd him!" The chief's eye flash'd; his plans
　Soar'd up again like fire.

The chief's eye flash'd; but presently
　Soften'd itself, as sheathes
35　A film the mother-eagle's eye
　When her bruis'd eaglet breathes.
"You're wounded!" "Nay," the soldier's pride
　Touch'd to the quick, he said:
"I'm kill'd, Sire!" And his chief beside,
40　　Smiling the boy fell dead.

NOTES AND SUGGESTIONS

1. What is the "incident" referred to in the title of this poem?
2. Describe, in your own words, the picture of Napoleon, given in the opening lines of the poem.
3. a. In stanza 2, note the abrupt manner in which Napoleon's thoughts are broken off.
   b. What effect has this, on the description of the ride that is given in the next four lines?
4. a. Why was the rider smiling with joy?
   b. In lines 17, 18 and 19, how does the poet emphasize the fact that the rider was only a boy?
5. a. In lines 31 and 32, note how much is told you in a few words, concerning the effect of the good tidings, on the leader.

b. Note the repetition in line 33; what, probably, are Napoleon's thoughts?

c. What other side of Napoleon's character are we shown in the lines that follow?

6. Note the sharp contrast between the two characters of the poem, the leader and the boy. What is the real theme of the story?

Explanatory Notes

Page 183, line 1—"Ratisbon"—a town in Bavaria on the Danube river. It suffered severely during the five days' fighting between Napoleon and the Archduke Charles of Austria, in 1809.

Page 183, line 11—"Lannes"— born 1769, died 1809; he was a celebrated French marshal.

THE SONNETS

BY WILLIAM SHAKESPEARE, JOHN MILTON, WILLIAM WORDSWORTH, AND LORD BYRON

THE sonnet, a literary form copied from the Italian, was introduced in England about the middle of the sixteenth century by Sir Thomas Wyatt and the Earl of Surrey. It became popular immediately and ever since has been used at times by nearly all the great poets.

The sonnet is a poem of fourteen lines and has for its theme some topic that may be completely treated of in that space.

There are two forms. In the first, the fourteen lines are divided into three stanzas of four lines each with alternate lines rhyming and a final rhyming couplet. This is the form of sonnet adopted by Shakespeare and used throughout his sonnet sequence. In the second, the poem is divided into two parts, consisting of eight and six lines respectively. The first eight lines are closely bound together by the rhyme scheme which is uniform and may be indicated in the following way: "a b b a a b b a." In regard to the final six lines there is no uniform rhyme scheme. In both forms of the sonnet, the lines consist of ten syllables, the accented one following the unaccented one.

SONNET

BY SHAKESPEARE

O, HOW much more doth beauty beauteous seem,
By that sweet ornament which truth doth give!
The rose looks fair, but fairer we it deem
For that sweet odour which doth in it live.
5 The canker-blooms have full as deep a dye
As the perfumed tincture of the roses,
Hang on such thorns, and play as wantonly
When summer's breath their masked buds discloses:
But, for their virtue only is their show,
10 They live unwoo'd, and unrespected fade;
Die to themselves. Sweet roses do not so;
Of their sweet deaths are sweetest odours made:
And so of you, beauteous and lovely youth,
When that shall fade, by verse distils your truth.

NOTES AND SUGGESTIONS

1. What is the thought expressed in the first two lines?
2. E x p l a i n the comparison made in the third and fourth lines.
3. a. How do the canker-blooms differ from the roses?
b. What happens to them?
c. What becomes of the roses when they die?
4. Explain the last two lines.
5. Note how melodious the verses are.
6. a. Point out the rhyme scheme.
b. What meter is used?

SONNET
(On His Blindness)

BY JOHN MILTON

WHEN I consider how my light is spent
Ere half my days, in this dark world and wide,
And that one talent which is death to hide,
Lodged with me useless, though my soul more bent

5 To serve therewith my Maker, and present
   My true account, lest he returning chide;
   "Doth God exact day-labor, light denied?"
   I fondly ask. But Patience, to prevent
   That murmur, soon replies, "God doth not need
10 Either man's work or his own gifts; who best
   Bear his mild yoke, they serve him best: his state
   Is kingly; thousands at his bidding speed,
   And post o'er land and ocean without rest;
   They also serve who only stand and wait."

NOTES AND SUGGESTIONS

1. a. Look up the facts about Milton's life.

  b. How was his blindness brought on?

  c. What great religious and political movement was he closely connected with?

2. Point out the differences in form between this sonnet and the sonnet of Shakespeare which precedes this.

3. Compare the two sonnets as to the subject matter.

4. a. Express, in your own words, the question that Milton asks himself.

  b. What is his answer to the question?

ENGLAND AND SWITZERLAND, 1802

BY WILLIAM WORDSWORTH

Two Voices are there; one is of the Sea,
One of the Mountains; each a mighty voice:
In both from age to age thou didst rejoice,
They were thy chosen music, Liberty!

5 There came a tyrant, and with holy glee
Thou fought'st against him,—but hast vainly striven:
Thou from thy Alpine holds at length art driven,
Where not a torrent murmurs heard by thee.

—Of one deep bliss thine ear hath been bereft;
10 Then cleave, O cleave to that which still is left—
For, high-soul'd Maid, what sorrow would it be
That Mountain floods should thunder as before,
And Ocean bellow from his rocky shore,
And neither awful Voice be heard by Thee!

NOTES AND SUGGESTIONS

Wordsworth was one of the English writers who had for a time, at least, been greatly influenced by the French Revolution. Although his attitude toward that movement changed somewhat, he was always a warm advocate for freedom in matters of government. He would naturally, then, become a bitter opponent of the French Empire established by Napoleon.

1. a. "Two Voices"—explain this.
   b. Which one of them is of the Sea? Which, of the Mountains?
2. The tyrant referred to in line 5, is Napoleon.
3. In the first eight lines what are we told concerning one of these voices?
4. Explain the last six lines.
5. a. Line 11, "high-soul'd Maid" —who is meant?
   b. What figure of speech is this?
6. Which form of sonnet has Wordsworth adopted, the Shakespearean or the Miltonic?

"THE WORLD IS TOO MUCH WITH US"

BY WILLIAM WORDSWORTH

THE World is too much with us; late and soon,
Getting and spending, we lay waste our powers;
Little we see in Nature that is ours;
We have given our hearts away, a sordid boon!

5 This Sea that bares her bosom to the moon,
The winds that will be howling at all hours
And are up-gather'd now like sleeping flowers,
For this, for everything, we are out of tune;

It moves us not.—Great God! I'd rather be
10 A Pagan suckled in a creed outworn,—
So might I, standing on this pleasant lea,

Have glimpses that would make me less forlorn;
Have sight of Proteus rising from the sea;
Or hear old Triton blow his wreathéd horn.

NOTES AND SUGGESTIONS

1. From what you have read of Wordsworth, w h a t phase of his nature does this poem show?

2. In the first eight lines, he finds fault with people for what?

3. a. Note the unusual beauty of some of the lines.
   b. Explain the figurative language in lines 5, 6 and 7.

4. What is his conclusion about the matter; he sets it forth in the last six lines.

Explanatory Notes

Page 189, line 13—Proteus—In classic mythology, a sea-god who had the power of assuming different shapes.
Page 189, line 14—T r i t o n— In Greek mythology, the son of Poseidon. He dwelt in a golden palace on the bottom of the ocean. He is usually represented with a horn.

COMPOSED UPON WESTMINSTER BRIDGE

BY WILLIAM WORDSWORTH

EARTH has not anything to show more fair:
Dull would he be of soul who could pass by
A sight so touching in its majesty:
This City now doth like a garment wear

5 The beauty of the morning: silent, bare,
Ships, towers, domes, theatres, and temples lie
Open unto the fields, and to the sky,—
All bright and glittering in the smokeless air.

Never did sun more beautifully steep
10   In his first splendor valley, rock, or hill;
Ne'er saw I, never felt, a calm so deep!

The river glideth at his own sweet will:
Dear God! the very houses seem asleep; /
And all that mighty heart is lying still!

NOTES AND SUGGESTIONS

1. a. What is the theme of this sonnet?
  b. Why is the theme suitable for poetry?
2. a. What time of day is it?
  b. Explain the intense calm and quiet and yet the brightness of the morning.

3. Note especially the beauty of the last three lines.
4. Explain the line—"the river glideth at his own sweet will."
5. What figure of speech in the last line?

ON THE CASTLE OF CHILLON

BY LORD BYRON

ETERNAL Spirit of the chainless Mind!
Brightest in dungeons, Liberty! thou art,
For there thy habitation is the heart—
The heart which love of Thee alone can bind;

5   And when thy sons to fetters are consign'd,
To fetters, and the damp vault's dayless gloom,
Their country conquers with their martyrdom,
And Freedom's fame finds wings on every wind.

Chillon! thy prison is a holy place
10   And thy sad floor an altar, for 'twas trod,
Until his very steps have left a trace

Worn as if thy cold pavement were a sod,
By Bonnivard! May none those marks efface!
For they appeal from tyranny to God.

NOTES AND SUGGESTIONS

Lord Byron was born in 1788 and died in 1824. He was another of the writers of the early part of the 19th century who had been profoundly affected by the French Revolution. He became an ardent upholder of the rights of the people. His ideas on Liberty led him to aid the Italians in their struggle for freedom and later, he took a prominent part in the Greek war for independence, against the Turks.

This sonnet expresses very strongly, his fervent love of Liberty. It was inspired by a visit to the Castle of Chillon—a famous fortress at the Eastern end of Lake Geneva. Bonnivard, the heroic defender of Swiss liberty against the Duke of Savoy, had been kept a prisoner in a dungeon of the castle for six years (1530–1536). Byron used the same theme for one of his long poems, "The Prisoner of Chillon."

1. What is the "Eternal Spirit of the chainless mind"?
2. Why is Liberty brightest in dungeons?
3. Explain the lines, 5 through 8.
4. Explain the figure of speech in line 10.
5. Note the strength of the closing lines.

PATRIOTIC HYMNS

CONCORD HYMN

(Sung at the completion of the Battle Monument, April 19, 1836)

BY RALPH WALDO EMERSON

By the rude bridge that arched the flood,
Their flag to April's breeze unfurled,
Here once the embattled farmers stood,
And fired the shot heard round the world.

5   The foe long since in silence slept;
      Alike the conqueror silent sleeps;
      And Time the ruined bridge has swept
      Down the dark stream which seaward creeps.

      On this green bank, by this soft stream,
10   We set to-day a votive stone;
      That memory may their deed redeem,
      When, like our sires, our sons are gone.

      Spirit that made those heroes dare
      To die, and leave their children free,
15   Bid Time and Nature gently spare
      The shaft we raise to them and thee.

NOTES AND SUGGESTIONS

1. What historical event does this poem commemorate?
2. What was the occasion of its publication?
3. Explain "embattled farmers."
4. Explain line 4.
5. Point out the lines that seem to you to be especially beautiful.
6. a. What is the prayer of the poet in the last stanza?
   b. To whom is it made?

RECESSIONAL

BY RUDYARD KIPLING

      God of our fathers, known of old—
      Lord of our far-flung battle line—
      Beneath Whose awful Hand we hold
      Dominion over palm and pine—
5   Lord God of Hosts, be with us yet,
      Lest we forget—lest we forget!

The tumult and the shouting dies—
  The captains and the kings depart;
Still stands Thine ancient sacrifice,
10   An humble and a contrite heart.
Lord God of Hosts, be with us yet,
Lest we forget—lest we forget!

Far called our navies melt away—
  On dune and headland sinks the fire—
15 Lo, all our pomp of yesterday
  Is one with Nineveh and Tyre!
Judge of the Nations, spare us yet,
Lest we forget—lest we forget!

If, drunk with sight of power, we loose
20   Wild tongues that have not Thee in awe—
Such boasting as the Gentiles use,
  Or lesser breeds without the law—
Lord God of Hosts, be with us yet,
Lest we forget—lest we forget!

25 For heathen heart that puts her trust
  In reeking tube and iron shard—
All valiant dust that builds on dust,
  And guarding calls not Thee to guard—
For frantic boast and foolish word,
30 Thy mercy on Thy people, Lord!
               AMEN!

NOTES AND SUGGESTIONS

1. Express, in your own words, the theme of this poem.
2. Explain line 4.
3. Explain the figures of speech in lines 7 and 8.
4. What are the thoughts expressed in stanza 4?
5. a. Point out lines or passages that seem to you to have unusual beauty.
   b. Give your reasons for thinking so.
6. What is the significance of the title of this poem?

Lightning Source UK Ltd.
Milton Keynes UK
UKHW020636100521
383440UK00002B/4